LIES, LEG LOCKS, AND THE BACK HOOK SPIN

LEIGH DONNELLY

ISBN: 978-1-7362068-6-7

For the amazing crew at Studio Spin.

HOW IT BEGINS: CALISTA

The first five minutes are tricky. For one, I'm more than slightly achy today, and the familiar feeling of fatigue is kicking in, so the walk to Rat Rock in Central Park is at a slower pace than I'm used to. Much more glacial than the pace of our teenage selves a few decades back. The other oddity of it all is the feel and sound of the paper bag crinkling around the Mad Dog 20/20 I'm illegally taking into the park so that Paige, my old college roomy, and I can properly enjoy the nostalgia attached to this outing.

"Ugh, it's so gross," Paige says once we've met up at our sacred meeting place: one of the lower rocks where we have a good view for people watching but are not on prominent display ourselves. Her face distorts as some of the blood-red liquid trickles down her chin.

I agree. It's vile compared to my usual bougie wine selection, but I'm quite the drinker now that I'm regularly self-medicating my various pains, so I take a large swig and enjoy the burn at the end, knowing it's going to quickly provide some much needed relief since I skipped lunch. Drinks on an empty stomach beats waiting for an aspirin to kick in.

"So, Tiny Dancer, I've been following your studio on Insta.

Looks like it's thriving under your leadership," Paige says, now unaffected by the taste of her Mad Dog as she takes her own generous gulps.

I smile at the mention of my old nickname. Given to me because I was a dancing major surrounded by students studying to be publicists, human resources managers, accountants, and other corporate-related positions. My head buzzes pleasantly from the fond memories of college all those years back, from the relief of this escape where I have alcohol, from the feel of the warm rock and the May sun after a long winter, and from the company of an old friend that I haven't seen in years. *Yes, I am still Tiny Dancer,* I tell myself.

"I'm actually working on opening a second location," I say, still basking in the good vibes of the present company and surroundings. "Somewhere in Chelsea or around there. Nothing too far from where I already am."

Paige, ever the optimist about what her friends can achieve, raises her hands and gives an impromptu dance of sorts as she sloshes Mad Dog on the rock where we're perched.

I don't enjoy telling people, regardless of how well I know them, about my latest health struggles. That's what I call them: health struggles. Anyone who doesn't have them doesn't understand. They try to, but often the more it negatively affects friendships, romantic relationships, or working relationships, the more difficult it is for them to find and keep their empathy.

In the cab on my way over, I went back and forth on whether I would tell Paige about my health struggles and how I needed help with the studio because of that, or if I would partially lie and say my troubles were stemming from trying to open a new location. Even when we sat down and started chatting, I wasn't sure which narrative I would go with. Looks like my buzzed mind decided for me. Probably because I didn't want to ruin the vibes we had going. The booze placated my pain. Why bring it up again when it was more fun talking about a potential second location, something that had been an actual plan in the not too distant past?

So I go with it. We excitedly talk about which parts of Chelsea would work best, and I'll need to change my marketing techniques to a reach a slightly different audience than the one I'm currently appealing to on the outskirts of the Theater District.

I'm just over forty, but I feel like I'm twenty again, dreaming about what my future could hold with no consideration for whether my body and mind will be healthy enough to allow it. Because at this moment on the rock, both feel completely intact. My brain, even with the alcohol, feels sharper than it has in weeks, and my pain has receded into the background. Never fully gone, but mild enough that I can focus on other things outside of my discomfort. And even though my fatigue is forever present, sitting down during this discussion allows me to pretend it doesn't exist.

"What month are you planning for the ribbon cutting?" Paige asks. She's finished her drink and now both hands have her phone out, her calendar app pulled up. "I'll block out the entire month now. I won't miss this one."

She's referencing the first studio opening, the one I botched seven times with delays, bank issues, and other variables often outside of my control. By the time I got it all sorted, I only had a week's notice to give to people and accidentally scheduled it the same day as my brother's high school graduation. It's a shame there won't be an actual second location. Not anytime soon, at least. I would like to have another shot at an opening day. I've learned so much since then.

"I don't know yet," I say, my hands playing with the paper bag, bending and then unbending the top edges as I talk.

Paige's smile drops, understanding there's more to the opening of a second studio, and it's likely not good.

"I'm having some financial issues." This part is true.

But what I leave out is that my financial issues are coming from my influx of very expensive medical bills. Turns out having lower abdominal pain that could be digestive or reproductive in nature, along with random severe headaches with no clear triggers, major fatigue that comes and rarely goes, foggy mental states that are just as sporadic, and a slew of other issues that may or may not be all related to each other doesn't point to any one clear disease or health issue. All it does is force doctors to run test after test (some of which may yield false positives or negatives), to question my understanding of my body and how it works, and to question my ability to adequately rate my pain (surely it can't be over four on a daily basis). The costs of the various tests and visits and overnight stays have depleted my checking and savings accounts.

"I had no idea," Paige says before looking around at the park and down at our empty bottles, still nestled in their brown bags. "Is that why we're illegally drinking Mad Dogs in the park? I'm all for it," she adds hastily, not wanting to sound like a snob. "I'm just curious. No judgment from a fellow poor person, I assure you."

I cock my head towards my empty bottle. "That was just on a whim. Recreating our childhood kind of thing. But the money issues are enough that I'm putting the second location on a brief hiatus and looking through my financial statements to figure out where the problem is."

Her eyes widen. "Is someone stealing from the company? From you?"

I shrug. It's the first time I've said anything about it to anyone besides a boyfriend who's no longer in the picture anyway, and suddenly I'm uncomfortable hearing it out loud. I feel my voice shrinking inside me when I go to answer her.

"Calista, you can tell me."

When we first arrived, we were giggly from the booze and the excitement of seeing each other after such a long hiatus. I didn't mean to bring us down this dreary road and wish I hadn't. But I need to talk to someone about it. And since Roderick left me a few weeks back, Paige is the only one left on my list of people I trust with my life who don't work with or for me.

"Everyone has always been like family at the studio. Hell, Luke *is* family. But there's money missing. I know it." This part is also true. I think. Once the bills started to literally pile up on my kitchen table, I took a hard look at everything related to my finances and they're not adding up. I wouldn't have caught it without the need to look for it, and now I'm wondering how long it's been going on. Like I told Paige, I've trusted everyone at the studio like family. It's naïve, but it's also not surprising for someone who never studied business and mostly was winging it for the past so many years.

"Shit," Paige says. She leans back against the rock, conveniently shaped similar to a chair with a slanted back. Perfect for getting a tan back when that was our sole reason for public day drinking in Central Park.

"Yeah, shit," I agree, matching her position. It's not nearly as comfortable as it was way back when. Getting old sucks.

"What now?" Paige asks. "Did you confront your staff about it?"

I watch the clouds slowly moving through the sky. This conversation should stress me out, but the alcohol on my empty stomach is doing its job well. I inhale deeply through my nose and let it out through my mouth. I can feel Paige beside me, hear her deep breaths concurrent with my own. It feels safe.

"No. I tried a few times, but I could never find the words; I couldn't risk ruining everything by saying the wrong thing or accusing the wrong person. According to Google, my primary source of direction for how to run a business, I should contact the police or a private investigator. Both things I'm loath to do."

"Shit," she says again. "That's… intense."

"Yeah. Both mean I have to let some stranger into the studio and trust they won't fuck up the dynamics. You know, make my staff or clients uncomfortable while they look at all the processes I have in place, all my files, everything.

"I know that's what some businesses do every now and then; standard operating procedure sort of thing. But it's not how I do things. And that was the whole point of opening my own studio. I wanted to be Frank Sinatra and do it my way."

I close my eyes and I can see the cops or investigators in my mind. Everyone would be having a chill, Zen day in the studio, a place that was made for exactly that purpose. And then, some man or woman in a suit would walk in and start snooping around and scrutinizing everything. The staff would tense up, which would make the students tense up.

They'd start with Florence at the front desk. Watching her every move as she entered client information, generated schedules, and ran payroll. All the while, she would in kind get snippy as hell with them. Especially if it was a man invading her space.

Luke, my brother, would be the worst about it. Our family had issues with money and distrust and greed. We'd actually made a pact years ago never to let money get between us. Shook on it and everything. If I even hinted Luke was a suspect along with everyone else, that I thought he was doing something incorrectly, much less immorally or unethically, it would destroy our already tense relationship. Conversely, I couldn't hire an investigator or get the cops involved and direct them to not investigate anything Luke was doing. It would defeat the purpose.

I explain as much to Paige and she makes the standard interjections to show she agrees and understands.

We both watch the clouds pass by overhead. Quiet for the moment while we contemplate what was said and if there's any reasonable solution to the problem at hand.

"I could do it," Paige says with the confidence of someone who is just buzzed enough to believe most things are possible if only you try hard enough.

I picture this new scenario of Paige, whom some of the staff–Luke included–know and trust, coming in and poking around. She wouldn't wear a suit; she wouldn't be rigid and informal and without personality. And I trust her with my life. But no, it still won't work.

I shake my head and sit up. The pain in my gut is mild, but I still give a quick sigh in relief that it's not worse. It varies not only day by day but hour by hour. My hand instinctively rests on my lower stomach, a pre-emptive move, since I expect to feel cramping and bouts of pain at any moment.

"You would be fabulous, and I love you for offering. But the problem comes as soon as there's an obvious investigation," I say, looking over to Paige, who is now repositioning herself, so she's sitting upright, too. I take another deep breath. What I want to say is that I've been an absolute mess for the past half year or so. My pain makes me irritable and I've started snapping at people. Then I started drinking. My face reddens at the thought of how before I started calling out, I tried having a few drinks before work. I wasn't outright drunk, but it was a 180 from the version of myself the crew and clients were used to seeing.

"There's tension at work," I end up saying as a version of the truth. I'm speaking to my feet, studying the pedicure I got two weeks back after the first nice spring day. "I can't do anything that shows a me-versus-them situation. Things are complicated."

It's the magic term for us that started in college. When we're talking and don't want to elaborate on something, we'll just add that it's complicated and the other person knows nothing more will be said about the subject. No further explanation will be given, so don't even ask.

Paige nods in understanding and I scold myself for letting our friendship fall to the wayside over the past decade or so. For being so involved with my work and myself that we slipped into a friendship of occasional texts and sharing funny TikToks.

"So you need someone to go undercover at work? Investigate everything without anyone knowing that's what they're doing?"

I let out a laugh at the absurdity of it. "Yeah, an undercover pole dancer. That's exactly what I need. Know where I can find one?"

Paige is up in a heartbeat and pulling me up with her. The seemingly innocuous act sends pain jolting through me, but I make sure I'm turned away from her when I bend over and mouth *fuck*. A breath later, it subsides and I'm upright again with what's hopefully a normal-looking expression on my face. Though my hand will be glued to my lower stomach for at least the next 15-20 minutes.

Paige doesn't notice. Her eyes are wide, and her hands are up and animated as she's speaking. "I know the perfect person! Come on. We'll go back to my place to change–something more apropos for the mission at hand–then we're going to Times Square for drinks."

CHAPTER 1
ANNA: FRIDAY, MAY 24TH

"I was just in Italy, too. What a coincidence," I say to an eight-top table of women in their thirties. I've never left the East Coast, but I recently read *Inferno* (thanks to a random customer who left multiple Dan Brown paperbacks in my section a few months back) and have seen *Under the Tuscan Sun* more times than I'd like to admit. Surely I can handle some small talk about touristy shit around Italy.

Two decades ago, when I was an aspiring actress, I had actual characters I'd take on at restaurants, perfecting my accents, motivations, and backstories as I worked the tables before running off to an audition. Now? I'm a 39-year-old server who's given up on acting and anything else remotely related to the industry. The stories I currently tell are to help me keep my sanity and pay my rent.

"Really? What'd you think of Pompeii? That was our favorite." The red head is beaming back at me, ready to spout off every fact she can remember about the excavated ancient city that was never mentioned in my semi-academic resources. I vaguely remember a class in high school where the teacher rolled out the TV on wheels and we watched some sort of PBS special about it, but I spent most of that time writing gossipy notes to my friends and staring at the super-handsome-by-teenaged-girl-standards Chris Jones who sat a few seats in front of me.

Time to switch tactics.

"I was mostly there for skiing," I say after eyeing up the table and deciding they're not the skiing type. What does the skiing type look like? Fuck if I know, considering I've never been, but skiers and snowboards have a vibe, and I can feel it in my bones that these folks don't have it.

They're disappointed for all of a second before they eagerly start to talk over each other, reminiscing about that crazy week in Italy and how Molly, the wild one of the group, had a torrid affair with Matteo, their tour guide. Why not? She was recently divorced; she deserved to have a little fun.

As I listen with rapt attention, I do what I can at the table to clear plates and tidy up, my eyes only occasionally darting off to check the status of my other tables. In my mind, I pretend I'm merely cleaning up to help our server as I imagine that I'm a part of this tight-knit group. I suspend disbelief, and in my imagination I cosplay as a person who has the time and the means to schedule bi-annual holidays with my besties where we travel around the globe.

Most of the people I work with do not lie their ass off, or at the very least they lie only sparingly to where no one would ever flat-out call them a liar, but I still stand by my tried-and-true tactic of using fabricated stories. I have my reasons, and they're not entirely mercenary.

Yes, sometimes I lie to help form a connection with the restaurant guests, a shameless ploy to increase my tips. But just as often, I do it to make my nights more interesting with conversation that goes beyond "Would you like to try our famous Limoncello Strawberry Cocktail or an order of our decadent garlic bread knots?"

Sometimes I lie as a matter of self-preservation. It's hard to keep faking enthusiasm year after year within the same four walls of Papa Pizzano's Pizza Palace. Some days it's damn near impossible to share or at least match the excitement of the tourists coming through, one bus-load at a time, a never-ending revolving door of people who are out there living their best lives and exploring the world, while I rarely leave the city, much less the state.

This group is different. My enthusiasm is genuine because I can almost see myself in them. I'm not lying to them just for the tips. My fibs with them are a way of pretending, just for the course of a meal, that we are the same and I'm not disgustingly jealous–especially of Molly. Matteo sounds like a fucking god and when I pull out my vibrator tonight, I know damn well I'll be picturing him giving me the best sex of my life. Our bodies rocking below deck as our boat heads out to the island of Ischia where he'll then treat me to a private romantic dinner overlooking the water.

Inappropriate fantasies about their former lovers aside, it's safe to say we've grown as close as a server and customers can before things get too weird. I now have about 5-10 minutes left to put aside my daydreams and make sure I'm charming enough to earn the above-25% tip I so desperately need to continue living in this expensive-as-fuck city.

"Ladies," I say with my warmest smile, which is not a lie in any way. The emotional connection was real, even if some of the content discussed was slightly fabricated. "It's been an absolute pleasure serving you all tonight. I hope you enjoy Drunk Shakespeare, but how could you not, right?"

As everyone gathers their things and takes turns putting their cards into the little electronic device that sits on each table, we continue chatting about Shakespeare and booze and how they go so well together. Molly talks about how Edward, the chief actor in tonight's performance, looks scrumptious, and she hopes he's not too drunk afterwards to perform for her in her apartment. Turns out she's the NYC native of the group.

I currently have one solid, ride-or-die best friend, but we're too broke and usually exhausted to take on even a fraction of what my customers are doing. And then there's Molly, having amazing stranger sex all over the world before gabbing about it with a table of besties over mimosas the next morning. Molly's likely a few years younger than I am, but I want to be her when I grow up.

When we finally say our last goodbyes and the women hurry off to make their show, I notice the back of a head I would recognize anywhere, especially since the person at the bar is wearing one of my wigs. What can I say? I took the whole actress thing to the extreme: wigs, fake glasses, dummy casts, the works.

"Paige?" I call out to my neighbor, who happens to be my aforementioned best friend. "How much of that did you hear?"

When I'm waiting tables, I can't help but fully commit with a tunnel vision that could have me labeled as partially blind by some doctors. She could have been there all night and I'm only realizing it now.

Paige swivels around on the stool and I can see the woman has never properly worn a wig in all her life. Catching me eying up her fake locks, she puts a hand to the faux hair and looks to her friend who's also adorning one of my finest costume wigs.

"You're not mad, are you?" she says with a smile that tells me she's had a few drinks.

I shake my head. Paige and I exchanged keys a few years ago, and while we don't walk into each other's place daily, it's not entirely unheard of for us to pop by to borrow cups of sugar, random articles of clothing, and now hair, it seems.

"We tried our luck with alter egos tonight," her friend explained, her bright blue eyes sparkling under the chunks of brown plastic hair that won't stay put behind her ears. "We're not nearly as talented as you are, though."

"Agreed. *That* was a moving performance, Trix," she says, using my work alias. "Have *you* thought of trying out for Drunk Shakespeare? You're a natural."

"I'm too good for them," I say in a rare lie to Paige. I've tried out three times and been rejected, but Paige doesn't know that. Some failures are best kept to myself. "So, what really brings you two to Papa Pizzano's Pizza Palace? Aside from trying out my costume wigs and aliases as a form of cheap entertainment."

"We're in need of your services. Trixy, I want to introduce you to my old college roommate, Calista."

I slide my tray under my arm so I can shake Calista's hand even though it feels slightly off given the context of the situation: we're surrounded by garish faux Italian bric-a-brac and people stuffing their faces with American-style pizza, not in some boardroom with professionals closing a million dollar deal.

Paige, the queen of cutting right to the point, gets to it: "Calista here has a proposition for you."

My eyes move back to Calista, who is blatantly checking out my legs. While I'm usually damn close to being a savant at reading people and situations, I have no idea what is going on here. Or rather, I do have a small idea but refuse to believe it. Paige knows I'm neither a lesbian nor a sex worker.

Regardless, I'm suddenly self-conscious as I stand there in my short black skirt, red polo, and suspenders. I'm not sporting a wig tonight, but I suddenly wish I was. My light-brown, nothing-special hair is pulled back in a sloppy bun and my make-up job today is less than perfect, which is unusual for me.

"We won't discuss it here, of course," Calista says with a small playful laugh, further confusing me because it's sounding more and more like *that* kind of proposition. "Back at my place after your shift. I have a decent assortment of wines, and Paige and I will pick up some good food on our way back."

"Your place?" Now Paige is confused, too, and I can't tell if I'm relieved or more on edge.

"Is that okay? It's not far, and you haven't seen it in forever. I had poles installed," Calista says with a huge grin. "I can make content from my condo now!"

"I love that for you," a tipsy Paige says as she beams back at Calista.

"Thanks! It's everything I thought it would be. 10 out of 10, highly recommend."

I take in their conversation, feeling a twinge of jealousy that Paige has other friends. Then both women remember I still exist and turn back to me.

"Sorry," Calista says. "We haven't seen each other in person in a few years; we still have some catching up to do. In fact, I think we're going to settle up here and head back to my place for a quick tour. You'll come, too, right? Once your shift is over?"

"She's coming," Paige says with the confidence of someone who's perfectly buzzed. "I know you don't have plans." Her eyes dare me to lie and say that I do. "And you're going to want to hear Calista's *proposition*. I promise." She winks and adds, "I'll text you the address," as she pulls her phone from her purse.

Then I'm summoned by a guest at one of my booths. By the time I look over at them again, they're waving and heading out the door. For the next two hours I wonder what that was all about, and why I already know I'm going to Calista's condo in Hell's Kitchen, as soon as my shift is over.

CHAPTER 2
ANNA, FRIDAY, MAY 24TH

"Wow," I say as Calista welcomes me into her spacious condo, "this is gorgeous."

No lies were told. It has all the usual necessities with a kitchen, living space, and bedroom, but they're all regular sized like we're in some random suburb in middle America. There's even a balcony running the length of the condo, meaning there's enough room for multiple people to lounge on the various pieces of furniture scattered about out there. The balcony alone is more than half the size of my lowly apartment.

"Thanks," Calista says, all but brushing off the comment. She's changed into more comfortable clothing and her blonde hair is in a loose low ponytail. No sign of my wigs. "But I can't take much credit. It's all from inheritance money. The last of it, too, so now I'm working my ass off to keep it. Do you want some wine?" She's already in the kitchen, peering into a small wine fridge that sits under the island.

"Sure, whatever white you have is great. Thanks," I say reflexively, still taking in the view beyond the balcony and wondering what it would be like to wake up in this space every morning, with natural daylight, or in this case moon-light, streaming in.

Maybe I won't have to wonder much longer. I let my blind optimism run wild, trying to decide why I'm here and what kind of proposition Calista has for me. Maybe she wants me to switch living spaces with her for some crazy reason that wouldn't make any sense. Or maybe act as a live-in maid and chef even though I'm not super tidy and can't cook for shit. Still, if it's either or anything even remotely close to those, I'm in.

I notice a few telltale signs of a man cohabitating as well (a man's jacket hanging by the door, a pair of boxers peeking out from under the couch, and a Star Wars poster on the wall with signatures from the cast). It's unfairly sexist, and yet I'd bet my life that all three are the result of a male roommate or boyfriend. Not that Calista having a live-in beau would deter me in any way.

"Is Paige here?" I ask when it finally occurs to me that while I'm creating nonsensical, hypothetical reasons about why I'm here and who else might live here as well, I've completely overlooked the person missing from the scene.

"Up here!" I hear Paige call in a semi-drunk sing-song voice.

No. Freaking. Way. Tucked away behind the far wall is a staircase leading up to more square footage. It doesn't seem possible.

Calista hands me a stemless, filled-just-below-the-rim wine glass and leads the way up the industrial-looking stair-case. Over her shoulder she says, "I use the tiny guest bedroom on the main floor as my room. I repurposed the main bedroom upstairs to be my studio. Paige is up there with all the food. We weren't sure if you had anything at work or not."

"No," I lie. "I try not to eat the pizza if I can help it." While Calista has already admitted sheer luck is the reason she has such a luxurious place, I'm still not willing to admit I practically starve myself just waiting to get to work where I get a complimentary personal-sized pizza for each four-hour shift I work. She wouldn't judge me, I assume, but it takes a lot for me to fully let my guard down and we've only just met.

Once I turn the corner at the top of the stairs, I'm relieved I kept my abject poverty to myself. I feel like a peasant stepping into the room in my tattered t-shirt and old sweatpants I've converted into shorts, the sorry image complete with the well-worn sneakers I change into before making my way to or from work.

My gross, pizza-smelling self does not belong in this sacred space. The upstairs bedroom sprawls across the same footprint of the lower floor, but without any walls or barriers cutting up the space, barring the bathroom at the other end of the room. One outer wall running the length of the space is lined with ceiling-to-floor mirrors. The wall opposite sports a long couch that runs at least ten feet and stops abruptly on each end with no armrests. Paige looks relaxed on the couch; the ottoman in front of her is covered with a hard top and lots of bougie-looking hors d'oeuvres. In the middle of the room are two metal, vertical poles and special track lighting in the ceiling that puts different colored spotlights on each pole, the sight of which reminds me that I'm not here to take a tour of the local real estate.

"Calista, what exactly did you mean when you said you had a proposition for me?" I ask as I walk towards Paige. The food draws me in despite the voices in my head screaming *potential stranger danger* and *get out now*. I don't do either and instead have a seat next to my friend and immediately dig into the loaded bruschetta, wild-mushroom flatbread, and stuffed meatballs. There's not a doubt in my mind that if this is the end of me, I will die happy with wine and a belly full of delicious food. Besides, if Paige trusts Calista, so do I. Even if it looks like an unmarked white van should be parked out front.

"I'm officially out of options, and I need your help," Calista says, catching me by such surprise that I almost allow a rogue wild mushroom to slip off my slice of flatbread and onto the impeccably clean, light gray couch. Calista's taste in furniture is ballsy, to say the least.

Ignoring my near faux pas, Calista continues to detail out her current situation. "There are financial issues at the studio, my pole dancing studio, and I need someone's help; someone completely unknown to my staff. A person who can come in, befriend my employees and earn their trust, learn how everything works, and help me get to the bottom of it all."

I almost laugh into my wine. I really need to stop eating and drinking during this conversation. It will not end well for this couch.

"Me? You want me to come in like a spy? And do what, exactly? What are the issues?" A memory from a few hours earlier pops into my head. In the first hour of my shift, I lost my cool with two busboys. Instead of being the much older and wiser adult and helping them work out their disagreement, I'd encouraged them to settle it out in the alley. My manager, Diesel, had to send them both home for the night because their faces were all bruised and their knuckles bloodied. Too much gore for the front of a restaurant. How was I supposed to know they'd be dumb enough to actually have a mid-work fist-fight in the alley? Needless to say, I'm not sure I'm the right person for this job.

"Financial issues, I guess you could say." Calista looks to Paige for help in how to explain it all, but Paige is clearly just there for the food and booze. Being her neighbor and friend, I know she's just as broke as I am, so this doesn't surprise me.

"I'm almost positive there are a few bad players at the studio," Calista says, her bright blue eyes dimming slightly with the admission. "Money that should be there isn't. I have my own suspicions about who these people are, but I'd rather not share that with you just yet. Go in with clean eyes; maybe you'll pick up on stuff that I haven't even noticed."

This makes more sense to me. I didn't need to be an undercover spy at work to notice all the underhanded, shady dealings at the restaurant. It's because of the revolving door of staff there. When it's just a temporary job for and with people you don't give a shit about, it doesn't take much for people to dip into the tills, sneak food out the back, or pocket someone else's tips. While I can't see Diesel ever hiring a spy to root out the miscreants, I can understand that Calista and the studio are not an even comparison to Diesel and the pizza shop. Maybe this isn't as crazy as it sounds.

"Paige said you're an expert at telling just the right white lie to get people to open up to you," Calista continues, taking my silence as thoughtful consideration. "That's why we were at the bar tonight. I wanted to see your *acting* skills in person. Creating trust and putting people at ease is a must at our studio, given our biggest classes are the ones that involve pole dancing."

I'm… I don't know what I'm feeling. There's confusion about this entire scheme overall. But I'm also feeling slightly betrayed at Paige spilling my secrets, and defensive because I somehow feel like this is a criticism of my ethics regardless of how objectively Calista worded it.

"Paige also said you used to be a dancer. A serious dancer; you auditioned for Juilliard. The acting background, the story-telling, the dancing: it all makes you the perfect candidate to be my newest Pole 101 instructor slash undercover studio spy."

Luckily, I have nothing in my mouth to spit out or choke on. Instead, I stare at her dumbfounded, my head tilting slightly to the right as I take in what I've just heard.

"But I've never even touched a pole."

"I'll teach you," Calista is quick to say before I can finish declining.

She's leaning against one of the poles while Paige and I are sitting on the couch, and I wonder if her towering over us was a conscious or subconscious power move. Conscious, probably. Doubtful that Calista does anything accidentally.

"Honestly, give me a few weeks and you'll be a pro. It's what I do for a living and I'm damn good at it. I've already done the basic math in my head. Three weeks from now, if you practice a few hours a day with me, you can easily take over my class."

Seconds fly by and then Paige's hand is on my knee, giving it a quick squeeze in her excitement. "Oh my god, Anna, how are you not jumping at this? I wanted to do it, but she already knows I have a bum left knee and the rhythm of the forty-year-old white woman that I am. And I know some people who work there already, so they'd be weirded out that I was stepping in with zero experience. Too suspicious."

"I already have a job," I say weakly because even I can see that in terms of pay and overall job satisfaction, instructing pole at what is certainly a high-end studio is far better than serving at a chain pizza joint.

"It doesn't have to be one or the other. If you work mostly night shifts, I can train you during the day. And then you can switch your shifts to work around my already set Pole 101 class. Right? Isn't that one of the perks of waiting tables? Flexible schedule?"

She takes off her rings then shimmies out of her clothes, kicking them off to the side with her bare foot. Her toes accented with a lovely red pedicure that matches her pole outfit. I don't know what I expected a pole outfit to look like, but I was sure more glitter and less fabric would be involved.

That's not the case. The top resembles a sports bra in coverage and how snug it is, but there are extra straps over the shoulder and below around the ribcage, giving it a subtly sexy allure. The bottom is similar to underwear in what it covers, but again there are extra straps going down the thigh that meet and attach to a strap that circles around the mid-thigh area.

"Look, I'll show you the basic moves I teach to my students. I promise, it's rudimentary; not difficult at all for someone with your dance background. And since you were hauling those trays around, I'm sure you have the upper-body strength needed, too."

Calista taps her phone before tossing it gently onto her pile of discarded clothing; speakers from around the room play "Cough Syrup" by Young the Giant.

With the grace of a Paris Opera ballerina, she places one hand high on the pole, takes a few steps to gain momentum, and then her feet are off the ground. One leg wraps around the pole and both sets of toes are pointed as she spins, holding herself up with just an arm and a leg.

The beauty of it all might be the most surprising aspect of the night. The media outlets portray pole dancing as this dirty act that is only done in dark, filthy rooms where shame permeates the air in such thick waves it threatens to suffocate all who dare to partake in it. I feel my own guilt with my initial reaction to seeing the poles in the room and assuming the worst. I see now that windowless white vans have no business here.

Paige and I don't eat. We don't drink. We watch with rapt attention. I recognize in Calista's expression a feeling of contentment and inner peace, and I see my younger self in her.

The song finishes and the room is once again quiet, but we still don't hear Calista's toes and the balls of her feet recon-necting with the floor.

"That can't be all the moves of an intro class," I say. "Or if it was, now show me what an advanced class looks like."

Calista grimaces. I think I see her hand go to her stomach

and her shoulders slump ever so slightly, but then she gives a soft laugh and says, "You're right. I threw a few intermediate moves in there. Just wanted to give you a glimpse of what else is out there beyond the basics. The really advanced moves will have to wait. I've been drinking, so inversions aren't an option, but I will do a quick run-down of the specific moves. Only the basics this time. Promise.

"This is the back hook spin, this one is the stag spin, the fan kick, peek a boo." Calista is spinning, strutting, sliding, posing. It sounds like Catherine Zeta-Jones in *Chicago* describing her grand finale routine. Then the words fall off and only positions remain as she transitions from one move to the next using only muscle memory. Or maybe she practiced the routine out beforehand.

Her toes find the ground again. A perfect landing; though this time she's clearly out of breath. Casually, Calista sits on the floor, on the other side of the ottoman, and I again wonder if this is purposeful. I am now sitting higher than she is while she goes over the specific details of what she is asking me to do.

I won't be covering her classes as Anna Laurier, a friend of a friend. I'll be doing it as Jessica Brown, a more common name so that if someone tries to Google me, they'll be inundated with enough Jessica Browns they'd probably lose interest before even starting to sort through them all. It's important no one knows I have *any* connection to Calista. According to her, there's a divide of sorts at the studio, a disconnect between her and the staff, and I need to be on the right side of it, the employee side. With my current social media covered in pictures of Paige and me, being Anna isn't an option. Anna traces back to Calista via Paige.

I bite my lower lip, mulling this all over. It's not how things are done. Business owners don't generally hire fake employees to sneak around and spy on all the actual employees. It simultaneously feels so right and so wrong, and the wine is hitting my brain, and my body is itching to get on the pole and do everything Calista just did.

I'd thought about joining a local dance studio, but the cost has always been an issue. This gift of getting paid to be trained one-on-one by a professional and then getting paid to teach pole to others? This scenario will never present itself to me again. Ever. If I say no, I'll be lying awake in bed every night wondering why I'm not pole dancing and living my best life as Jessica Brown.

"I'll give you $5,000 up front," Calista blurts out. It looks almost like she surprised herself with the comment. "Block off three weeks of your calendar for training and promise me at least an additional four weeks of working and investigating in the studio."

I purse my lips together to hide any hint of a smile, but she can tell I'm ready to cave.

"There's another 10 for you when you can tell me who's stealing from the company," Calista says, knowing I'm teetering on the edge of agreement, and that money is the obvious path to a *yes* from me. "All cash. You'll also be paid hourly as an instructor, but that can't be under the table. I need this to look as authentic as possible. I'll put you on the schedule and in our email under Jessica Brown, and I'll handle the technical stuff on my side to make sure you're still paid and taxed properly under your real name."

I don't let my jaw drop, and I don't jump up to perform a celebratory dance, even though my blood is buzzing with excitement. Paige does it for me and demonstrates once and for all that she has zero moves as her arms and legs jerk about while her face contorts into that of a person possessed. It's endearing, regardless. My mother always told me to surround myself with supportive women.

Maybe it's the lure of the life-changing money, maybe it's Paige's infectious enthusiasm. I can't even list out all the ways this feels right deep in my bones. It's as if it's finally dawned on me that the past few years, decades, really, where I've felt like I'm merely going through the motions of life without any real purpose, it was actually all leading up to this moment, this opportunity.

Calista goes on with logistics and talks about a nondisclosure agreement she'll have her lawyer draft up. I listen and take it all in, knowing I'll sign without giving it another thought. So eager to begin my new life as Jessica Brown. Jessi for short.

CHAPTER 3
ANNA: FRIDAY, JUNE 28TH

t took a bit of maneuvering with schedules for both me and Calista, but all the hassle has been worth it. The last three weeks have been the best of my life.

Calista's classes, the one's I'll be temporarily taking over, all happen in the evening so she's been instructing me at her place for a few hours each day and then I get a quick break before heading into the restaurant for my evening shift.

When I first signed on to this crazy scheme, I'd stupidly compared myself to Baby in *Dirty Dancing*. If she could transform, before my very eyes, into a professional dancer in a matter of days, surely I could master the very basics of pole in a few weeks' time. According to Malcolm Gladwell, I was already a master dancer with well over 10,000 hours of targeted, grueling training under my belt. All I had to do was channel that knowledge into dancing with a vertical pole. Easy peasy.

I conveniently overlooked how I haven't truly danced in years. Even with my physically demanding job as a server, I'm out of shape, not nearly as flexible as I used to be, and overall I'm rustier than I'd realized.

And because my muscles ache at all times now and I'm more physically exhausted than maybe I've ever been in my life, I expected my tips to suffer accordingly. And yet, like a good omen confirming that this immoral side hustle was the right choice, my tips have only been increasing.

The crew at Papa Pizzano's Pizza Palace has noticed a change in me, too. I've heard some random comments and hushed whispers behind my back, while others have been bold enough to confront me head on.

"OMG, you're pregnant!" Helena says while she and I are picking up orders in the back kitchen, her jaw working overtime on a piece of gum she's chewing despite Diesel's strict rule against it.

"What? No! Not unless I'm the next virgin Mary." Not that anyone has ever made that comparison before. I'm usually fairly active in the bedroom, gathering most of my one-night stands via dating apps. But with all the extra work lately, there hasn't been time for anything beyond my little solo acts right before I fall into a deep and satisfying sleep each night.

"Huh," says Helena, her eyes narrowing and inspecting my belly. Fully aware she's scrutinizing me, I try not to show my discomfort and stiff muscles as I stand up with my loaded tray. "Well, something's different. Your face is all glowing, but in a good way. Not in a sweaty mess kinda way."

I can't believe it. Aside from when I'm "performing" for my tables, I'm usually accused of having massive resting bitch face. A condition I've been living with all my adult life But what Helena is saying must be true: the increase in tips, multiple people commenting on some sort of positive difference they can't put their finger on, the pep in my step despite my aches. I'm just that damn happy to be dancing and moving to the rhythm of something that it stays with me almost permanently now.

Dancing is what's been missing. I made it all of two and a half semesters in college before life happened and I needed to focus more on surviving than finishing up my dance major. I told myself it was fine. It was only a temporary hiatus. Then it wasn't. I gave up dancing, and in the process, I lost a tiny but oh so important piece of my soul. And the craziest part was that I didn't even realize it. I attributed my unhappiness and feelings of discontent to everything but that: being poor, seasonal depression, a nasty breakup, and so on. But it was dancing all along.

Though I admit the increase in cash flow certainly isn't hurting my mood, either. Previously, I'd endured unrelenting intrusive thoughts about how I was going to end up homeless and starving in an alley somewhere, a giant city rat one day consuming whatever they could scrounge off my skeletal corpse behind some dumpster. Those voices have quieted now that I have a dual income. Even better, I've started buying groceries again. There are edible items in my tiny fridge. I was even looking online for potential vacations in Europe, and after a bit of saving in the future, it's closer to a possibility than a pipe dream for me.

After my last practice with Calista, once she gave me the official clearance that I was competent enough to take over her intro classes, I went on an online shopping spree (which I could afford!) and bought a bunch of sexy pole outfits. All bold colors and straps everywhere, a bit of shimmer here and there.

It's likely the confidence of my new glow and my sexy pole outfit under my tank and shorty shorts that has me openly checking out the guy in front of me at the coffee shop on my way to my first official class. He's wearing an interesting combo of jeans and a casual suit jacket, the kind a professor would wear. A bit young–maybe in his twenties even–but I'm not looking for forever, so I don't concern myself with that.

Because the mere thought of this man instructing a literature class of some sort makes me weak in the knees. I can see him with his dirty blonde hair neatly styled, his face freshly shaved, lecturing a hundred students or so about how the Industrial Revolution impacted the literature of the time. The thought has me all kinds of light-headed with a slow warmth spreading in my lower stomach. I love intelligence and confidence in a man. Sure, he looks to be at least a decade and a half younger than I am, now that I'm really paying attention, but the jacket and glasses are aging him just enough that the possibility of a one-night-stand doesn't feel out of the question.

He orders two dozen doughnuts, and now I'm convinced he's a professor leading a small, intimate, evening discussion on a special topic he's been researching for months. Maybe he'll offer up a few free doughnuts to help draw in the crowd before he wows them with his stellar intellect and charm.

I'm up next. I quickly give my iced coffee order and name to the barista before sliding over to the pickup area, "Hot for Teacher" playing in my mind as I join the professor. He pockets his phone and our eyes meet.

"Late for your lecture?" I ask, as if we see each other all the time and I don't need to bore him with formalities like "hello" or my name.

He responds with a look of confusion, and I don't give him a chance to ask questions before I start explaining myself.

"I figured with your outfit, you're some kind of professor or something. You know, getting doughnuts for students about to sit through a long lecture."

More confusion along with a smidge of amusement. A dimple pops up and I'm a goner. It's all too adorable and only serves to scatter my already broken brain.

"You know…" I say, trying to explain myself while I'm suddenly at a loss for 99% of the words in the English language. "The suit jacket and jeans; you're the cool professor. Business on top and party below your belt."

On the bottom! My brain screams at me before throwing up

her hands and calling it a day. The phrase I was looking for was *on the bottom*. Business on top and party on the bottom. What the fuck is wrong with me?

I stop talking. He stops blinking. I'm pretty sure the world stops turning for a split second. Luckily, it defies Newton's First Law of Motion and rotates once more when he cracks the most dazzling smile.

"You think there's a party below my belt? That's what she said, right? I'm not hearing things?" he questions the barista as he reaches for the two boxes of doughnuts she's sliding across the counter.

"Mmmm hmmm," the barista says in confirmation. Then she calls "Anna!" as if we aren't the only two customers in the shop.

"I—" I say, but he cuts me off, waving my response away with his one free hand. The barista gives up on handing me the drink and instead sets it on the counter. But I can't reach for it yet. I'm too embarrassed to process how hands and arms work.

"I'm fucking with you. I know what you meant, like the mullet: business in the front and party in the back."

"Exactly." I beam back at him. My crush on this man increases tenfold with his ability to discern my nonsensical comments. To my surprise, he continues to chat while I successfully retrieve my drink and load it up with sugar and cream.

"For what it's worth, you're right. I am an instructor. But I assure you my lectures are succinct and I would never need to bribe students with doughnuts." He checks his watch and calls out to the barista, "Thanks, Tabitha," before he gives me a quick nod and is heading out the door.

"See ya, Party Below the Belt," Tabitha says, with a shit-eating grin.

"Oh, no, Tabby. Can we not? Please?"

"I don't make the rules," she says, not at all sorry.

"Thanks for that," he says to me with a wink and half-smile before backing out the door and out of my life.

It's just as well. I'm in the midst of my rebranding as Jessica Brown, pole dancer extraordinaire. For weeks I've been reminding myself that once I walk into that studio, Anna Laurier ceases to exist. I am now Jessica Brown, and Jessica Brown doesn't get sidetracked by a random hot dude who gave her the slightest bit of attention, so neither do I.

Once that's settled, I head toward the studio and lock in my focus on my upcoming class. Thanks to Calista, I'm confident in the basic moves, but I need to learn the ins and outs of how to run one of the classes by taking one myself. While the other students will be focused on how to do the spins and where to put their arms and legs, I'll be zeroed in on even the tiniest of details about how the instructor is running the course and presenting each move. I've already seen how Calista does it when she trained me, but I'm excited to get another perspective on it.

"Hi there!" the receptionist says when I walk into the studio. She has gray hair stylishly falling to just above her shoulders and bright red lips. Each arm is covered in various tattoos that start at her wrist and continue until they disappear under her top. "What class are you here for?"

"Pole 101." While she looks through her paperwork, I admire the photos on the wall behind her, reminiscent of Sardis where I had the pleasure of eating once a decade or two back. Each photo is black and white and pops against the Barbie-pink colored accent wall. The instructors are spotlighted in the photos, each doing a different pole move or position. Their signature is in hot pink ink and is only sometimes legible, much like the signatures of most artists.

"Huh," says the receptionist. Florence, according to her name tag. "I don't see an Anna on our list for today's class. Did you register online?"

Shit. My cup has my real name on it. Seconds into my top-secret mission and I walk into the place with my real name plastered on my drink. Turns out casually lying as a server might be a little different from taking on a long-term alter ego and attempting to create long-term relationships.

"My name's actually Jessi. I use pseudonyms at coffee shops." I lean in conspiratorially and add in a whisper, "A lot of weirdos out there."

Her eyes widen when she nods her approval, and it hurts my heart a little. Florence is easily in her sixties, if not older, and I imagine she's experienced or at least seen some pretty awful shit in her life to hear that sort of response and immediately confirm that it was a good call and not at all paranoid.

"There really are, aren't there? Okay, let's see… Oh, Jessica Brown? You're taking over Calista's 101, right?"

"That's me. Jessi for short."

"It's so nice to meet you! Calista's told us all about you." I know what she means by this because Calista's already given me a rundown of my fabricated pole background. She kept as much truth as she could while still making sure it was plausible that someone like me would get hired for a position like this. The truths: I have a strong dancing background. The fibs: I went to and graduated from Juilliard; I've been poling professionally for the past three years and just recently moved back to NYC from Doylestown, PA. I don't know shit about the random town she pulled out of her ass, but I did some Googling so I could sound coherent in case anyone brings it up.

"Damn," she says, looking over my shoulder. "I need to keep checking everyone in; no time for chitchat. You can head back and get started if you want while everyone else gathers in the chill room." She's referring to the waiting room of sorts where students hang out and get changed prior to the class.

"That would be great. Thank you." I double back and head for the alternate entrance to the pole studio where class will be held. I also ditch my drink, vowing not to make that mistake again.

"My pleasure! And feel free to grab a doughnut from behind the desk if you want a quick sugar boost before class. Just don't eat in the main room. Shoes and food are off-limits there."

The word doughnut catches my attention. Sure enough, sitting on a counter behind the desk where Florence is stationed, are two doughnut boxes from somewhere. I can't read the name from this angle. I roll my eyes at myself and give a light chuckle as I head into the room. This is New York City, home to *millions* of people and likely just as many coffee and doughnut shops.

Any concerns are quickly dismissed as I turn my attention back to the task at hand. To ease my nerves, I decide to play around on the pole for a few minutes before class. Remind myself that I am a badass pole bitch, ready to impress Mel, the woman I'll be shadowing for this lesson.

I've already done extensive stretching back at the apartment, partly to warm up and partly to release my first-day nerves. My tank and shorts discarded in one of the squares on a shelving unit in the back corner, I walk up to the nearest pole. My left arm held high above my head, I grip the pole, lean my hips out, and strut like I'm a model on a runway. That's it. That was all I needed to relax. From there, I'm gliding around the pole. My left knee hooks for a move that's called the back hook spin. I can't focus on anything in particular while I'm spinning. One, because I'm spinning, and two because it's not second nature to me just yet and I need to concentrate on the minute details of what goes where and when. But as I'm slowing down and getting ready to make the softest landing of my life, I notice a man in the doorway wearing nothing but a pair of booty shorts and a smile.

My concentration breaks, my hands slip, and my knee grip slips. But I don't slip or slide. Instead, I flat out crash down into the floor, knees first. Fuck, I am way too old for that.

What hurts worse than my aching, over-thirty-five knees, is my pride when I see it's none other than the professor in the doorway. A look of concern only partially masking his amusement.

CHAPTER 4
LUKE, FRIDAY, JUNE 28TH

'm not sure what I was expecting when Calista randomly told me she'd hired someone new, someone I've never met. No, that's a lie. I'd expected a disaster. I love my big sister, but lately, she's been a mess of poor decisions: dating that ass hat Roderick, who walks around spewing bad vibes into whatever room he enters; her rush to open a second studio while the first can still take on more customers; her insistence that I, her in-house tech department, immediately install security cameras. It's all been so impulsive, everything within the last six months or so, when before that, things had been running smoothly for years.

I'm not a manager or anything, but as a sibling to the owner, I've been Calista's sounding board since before she even opened the place. Nothing was done without her running it by the family over dinner, and then eventually her running it by me over drinks when I was older. Once I was officially on the studio payroll, she always included me in the interview process for new hires.

So yes, this random hire I'm only meeting now for the first time, this person I can't find a lick of evidence of online? It felt like yet another poor, gut-reaction choice. There's a decent age gap between my sister and me–she's 41 and I'm 24–so I concede that maybe it's a sort of mid-life crisis that I'll only understand when I'm a few decades older. But it's also highly plausible she's losing her mind just because.

Either way, I've been increasing my time here to keep an eye on everything since Calista's been so distracted. I've already been doing everything I can to squelch some concerns from the other instructors and staff; I'm sensing one or two are getting that tingly feeling in their gut that something is off, especially after Calista started snapping at people at work. I saw Florence looking up different studios on the main computer, scrolling through the images of the instructors working there, and I overheard Nautica and Lyric (two of our instructors with the longest tenure at the studio) whispering about how Calista seems off lately–irritable and hot-headed is how they described her after a class let out and the clients appeared less than satisfied with the 101 class they just took. It wouldn't surprise me if we lost a few instructors to other studios in the upcoming months if we don't start making positive changes around here.

So yes, given the shit show that's been happening at the studio this year, I admit my first impression of Jessi (whom I could have sworn was named Anna at the coffee shop) was not a good one.

And I'm not referring to that adorable interaction in the cafe. Jumbling over conversations or suddenly being unable to form words is a common occurrence with me, too. I get it. And fuck did I almost ask her out right there at the counter, that shade of pink creeping up and turning those cheeks a bright red? Very sexy.

I'm talking about my first impression in the studio when I walked into my class, assuming the worst. When I startled her and sent her knees-first down to the floor, I almost chuckled at how predictable the whole thing was. How I'd correctly guessed, with little evidence to back it up, that the rando Calista hired would be a flaming dumpster fire of a disaster.

I see just how wrong I was mere minutes into the class, as I experience firsthand what Calista must have seen when she interviewed Jessi. The woman is decent enough on the pole, but it's her people skills that are blowing me away. Calista's always said that we can train just about anyone to be a pole dancer, but we can't teach people how to be patient, intuitive, and creative instructors. On that, we both agree.

I came into the building with my usual Friday-night delivery of two dozen doughnuts (because I always seem to lose the monthly studio bets we have going) and while I was dropping them off at the desk, I overheard one of the incoming students talking about how she was having the worst day. She was on the verge of snapping at any moment. I lingered behind the desk, fiddling with the box while I eavesdropped. The woman, Ellen, I later learned when we did class introductions, was hoping this class would help her destress, though she doubted it because really nothing in her life was going right. When she went to take her wedding band off and it wouldn't budge, she almost lost her shit. Had one of the other women not intervened, I think she would have had the willpower and desire to gnaw her own damn finger off.

A lightbulb went off in my head. I knew then that would be my ultimate test for the new person. Pair them up with Ellen to see if they could tame the wild beast while said wild beast was trying something extremely difficult for the first time in their life.

Honestly, I wasn't trying to be cruel, and I warned Jessi ahead of time about what I was doing. Not that I was testing her, per se, but I told her I knew one student was having a difficult day and that I'd like her, the only other experienced poler in the class, to partner up with this student to make sure she had a positive pole encounter. The first class can be a make-it-or-break-it experience for some people.

Like a pro, Jessi agreed enthusiastically.

Now here we are, a little over halfway through the lesson and building up to our first big move, the fireman spin, and Ellen is having the time of her life. I need to focus on the other pairs of students who are just learning and don't have one-on-one professional attention at their poles at all times, but with every sweep of the room, I find my eyes lingering too long when I come to Jessi. Hopefully she assumes I'm closely watching her to make sure she's ready to fly solo for her next class, but I'm not fooling myself and I doubt I'm fooling her, either.

I've just demonstrated the placement of each foot and hand for the fireman spin, step by step, and I've demonstrated the move itself as slowly as I can three times through, so now the class is trying it on their own with the help of their partners.

While the students are practicing, I walk around observing and offering pointers, encouragement, and praise where I can. This time, I start with Ellen and Jessi. Ellen is hesitant as she stands next to the pole. It's a funny thing about learning this sport. Nothing about it is natural. People think it's intuitive: walk up to the pole, circle once, then bring up your knees and spin. When you first start learning though, it's a lot trickier than it sounds. The inside hand has to plant higher than the outside hand—and how high matters. When circling the pole, you're not walking with a perfect posture. Instead, you kind of dip your hip out as you're walking around, but not too much and not too little. Sweep with your outside leg, then hook one ankle on the pole while the other ankle hooks around the first ankle. Not to mention the biggest rookie mistake that's tricky to undo once it's in people's heads: most people grip the pole with their upper thighs rather than the pads on the inside of their knees.

It's a lot to take in even though the move itself lasts mere seconds once executed at regular speed.

"Inside hand up, other hand across," Jessi instructs with the perfect combination of confidence and encouragement in her tone. "You've got this. Johnny's going to lose his shit when he sees you doing a spin on your first night."

I think it's the Johnny part that gets to Ellen. She puffs up her chest, grips the pole, takes a big step, and off she goes.

It's not graceful. She's gripping with her thighs, and her ankle isn't holding any of her weight, so she slides down almost immediately, similar to the way Jessi collapsed not too long ago.

"Yes!" Jessi beams back at her, eliciting yet another smile from Ellen in response. I do the same. How can I not? Her excitement is infectious and there isn't a hint of patronage in her tone.

Ellen's brief smile quickly fades as she looks around the room. Another classic mistake made by every student I've ever had: never compare personal gains against what someone else is doing.

"Nope," Jessi says before I can beat her to it. "We're not comparing ourselves. Pole's a personal journey. It's just you and this metal beast in front of you. Tame it. Mount it. Try it again, and this time grip the pole with your knees instead of your thighs."

Ellen looks at me for confirmation. I nod and say, "You're getting it. You've already won the first battle of getting airborne." Then I step back. I don't want to interfere. I'm certain that by the end of class, Jessi will be able to take a quick video of Ellen properly executing the fireman spin, and I don't want to take that away from her. Jessi is the one who's getting Ellen there, not me.

Ellen's outgoing, strong-willed, and fierce. Jessi must have caught on to that from the get-go and responded in kind with her instructional style and word choice.

Even though I'm on to the next pair, I sneak a peek back at Jessi and Ellen from time to time. By the time I've finished meeting up with all the other pairs in the class, Ellen's got it. Her knee and ankle placement could still use a bit of work, but that sort of precision comes with lots of practice; it's not something anyone should expect to master on the first day.

What happened with the fireman spin is generally how the rest of the class went. I was 99% focused on what I was doing and instructing, but a small part of me was always aware of Jessi, and I'm not entirely convinced that's because I'm trying to verify whether Calista made a good hiring choice with her new instructor. She was golden within the first half of the class. I have to admit that me watching her for the past almost hour has everything to do with my increasing fascination.

This is not my usual behavior. When I was a poor college student begging Calista for a job, she made me swear I wouldn't fuck up the platonic, like-family vibes she had going on at the studio. A somewhat polite way of saying no sleeping with clients and no sleeping with coworkers. Ever.

I enthusiastically agreed since the thought honestly never crossed my mind. I was there to dance and do a job, and so was everyone else. I wasn't interested in messing anything up over a few good rounds in the sack. But surely inviting Jessi to stay for an after work drink as a sort of welcome to our Art of Spinning family isn't breaking any rules. Really, it would be rude not to.

I never stay after class for drinks. In fact, I rarely drink at all. Probably because I squeezed a life-time of heavy drinking into four years of college. But it looks like that's about to change tonight. While the students are all congratulating one another in the chill room as they gather their things, I pounce when I see Lyric, one of the other instructors, coming downstairs from her party. Her class ended about fifteen minutes earlier, but there's more involved in bachelorette parties and it takes more time to clean up afterwards. The leftover booze, for example, which I see there's one full bottle in her arms, practically buried under everything else. Typical Lyric, she's a one trip kind of woman even if it means that one trip is a horrific struggle that may or may not end up with everything falling to the floor.

"Lyric, let me help you with that," I say, already reaching for a precariously placed box limiting her field of vision. "I was thinking of inviting the new hire for a drink. You in?"

"I never turn down drinks, Luke. You know this."

I look over my shoulder and see Jessi still at the studio door, chatting it up with her classmates.

"Listen," I say, my voice low to keep the conversation between us, "I don't think Jessi knows Calista's my sister. I'd rather keep it that way, please."

Lyric gives me a look that says so many things, but all she physically says is, "Yeah, okay."

CHAPTER 5
ANNA, FRIDAY, JUNE 28TH

After class, I'm practically high, my bloodstream packed with serotonin, dopamine, endorphins, and oxytocin, my face all aglow from pure contentment. Hurt knees? What hurt knees? My body will undoubtedly remind me of the searing pain tomorrow, but for another hour or so, I'm ready to take on Everest. That's part of the reason I agree to an after-class drink with Luke and a few of the other instructors.

"Happens all the time with bachelorette parties," Luke explains as he pours a bit of bubbly into a plastic champagne glass and hands it to me. "They come loaded with all kinds of booze but never finish it. Then they drunkenly insist we keep the leftovers for ourselves and we don't fight it too much. Most times, it's probably best if they don't have anything else to drink."

"Pour mine to the rim, Luke. That last class was pumped; I've earned this," says Lyric, the instructor who took on the rowdy group of bachelorette party-goers. She pulls her long blue hair into a low ponytail while she waits for Luke to pour her drink.

The front door is locked, and the four remaining instructors, Luke, Lyric, Mel (short for Melody), and me, are now all fully clothed in whatever comfy clothing we wore on our way to the studio tonight. Luke and I are on opposite ends of the couch while the other two are each in a chair surrounding a coffee table. We're in the chill room, one of the small rooms designated for students who are waiting for classes to begin.

"Don't listen to her," Mel tells me, a smirk on her face. "Lyric loves those classes. She's a straight up hoe and her hoe energy is directly derived from all the penis straws, inflatable cocks, and edible chocolate dicks. Not to mention the songs. She feeds off all of it."

Lyric sighs and smiles first at Mel, and then at me. "She's right. I fucking love it. My own bachelorette party, almost a decade ago now, was one of the best nights of my life. Who wouldn't want to relive that every now and then?"

"Twice a week is not every now and then," says Luke.

And so it continues with the playful banter among coworkers as we sip on champagne that doesn't bite as it goes down. I chime in now and then where I can, but mostly I'm absorbing it all, especially Luke.

He's not wearing his glasses now, and he didn't during class either. I wonder if they're for reading, or fashion, or maybe he's blind as a bat but slipped in a set of contacts. Either way, he's stunning with or without them. And now, thanks to seeing him in nothing but a tiny piece of fabric, I know that under that professor-jacket is a decent-sized tattoo on his left pec, some sort of subtle flower that's mostly leaves and vine-like stems. I want to know what it is and what it means; I want to know what his chest feels like against my hands. I want to know a lot of things I probably shouldn't.

I'd gotten myself in a tizzy before at the coffee shop, imagining him commanding an academic class somewhere, but actually watching him lead a pole class was exponentially sexier than anything I could have dreamed up.

The students in class were all business. From the brief

chatter I heard during the introductory segment Luke started with, some were here for career purposes. They have aspirations of making it big in the stripper world. Some were here to regain their former, adventurous selves that wouldn't have thought twice about taking a pole dancing class a few decades back. And a few were here because they're like me. They just need *something* in their lives, and it felt like this might be it.

The room we were in for class is shaped like a rectangle with one long wall covered in mirrors. There are ten poles set up in two staggered rows of five, and the classes cap out at twenty students. Calista said they like to have people share poles, especially during the introductory classes. It promotes community with the other class members, allows for the students to help each other, and it prevents burnout and over-exertion since it forces people to take breaks while their partner has a turn.

The lights were dimmed during instruction. I've been told they do that to help ease anxiety. We're all in limited clothing so we can adequately grip the pole with our skin, but we're also standing around a bunch of strangers staring at mirrors, about to perform various moves that some would only do alone, in the comfort of their own home. For many people, this class setup would be a literal nightmare. The dimmed lighting helps deter our learned behaviors of cutting down our bodies with an inner monologue containing the most vitriolic comments known to humankind.

This is yet another reason I feel at home here, in this studio. This is what women were made for. To boldly be themselves and give zero fucks about the societal pressures that exist on the other side of the door. We were all sizes, with nothing to hide our true form, and by the middle of the class, every single person in the room dropped their crossed arms as we embraced existing just as we were.

I have to give Luke credit for this seemingly impossible

feat–a trick that's even more impressive given a good-looking man was in the room with all of us. He humbly admitted how some moves still hurt him, regardless of how he made it seem otherwise. He maintained a cool disposition throughout that kept everyone else calm and reduced any urges to panic. When he learned that Cyndi, one student in his class, was looking to take her stripper career to the next level, he was sure to give her pointers for how she could practice the moves at home in heels in between classes and which stretches she should focus on to master splits.

It was supposed to be Mel leading the class, but for whatever reason, Calista had them switch at the last minute. I don't know anything about how Mel teaches, but from the beginning, Luke set the zero-judgment tone. He was the reason some women who initially kept on additional articles of clothing decided to shed them, the reason their crossed arms finally relaxed at their sides. Fuck me, it was so hot watching him interact with everyone in that way.

I made mental notes of it all throughout the lesson. I already knew all of that thanks to my grueling three-week pole bootcamp class in Calista's condo. So I was only in Pole 101 as a student to learn the skills of leading a class of my own. I needed to know what to say and how to say it, what to do and how to present it in just the right way so everyone was comfortable and confident. There's a certain finesse involved in getting vulnerable students to trust the instructor enough to take the risks necessary to master pole dancing. I can only hope I'm half as good as Luke is.

Back in the chill room, Melody's face lights up as if something has just occurred to her, and from the tone of her voice, it's clear she's a little tipsy already. "Speaking of bachelorette parties… Do you all remember the time I had to cover Lyric's classes a few years back? Remember when that one group brought in an actual stripper who commandeered the class and put on a performance?"

This pulls me back to the present and pulls my eyes away from Luke.

"Yes, Mel, I remember getting mono and missing one of the craziest parties ever to come through the doors of Art of Spinning." Lyric looks at me. "She reminds me at least once a year."

"Maybe more," Luke adds, causing Lyric to give Mel a look that says, *See, even he agrees.*

I let my jaw drop, and Mel is practically giddy at my response. She's desperate to tell this story again to fresh ears, and I'm here for it. "I'm *dying* to hear this one, Mel."

At my encouragement to Mel, Lyric rolls her eyes and sets her empty glass on the table.

"Sorry," I say to her, though it's clearly just a formality. I'm not sorry enough to pass it up. Besides, there's a hint of a smile beneath her scowl. "Can I get you a refill? A little something to take off the sting?" I hold up the champagne bottle and tilt the top towards her, a peace offering of sorts. Lyric's pretense of being annoyed drops as she raises her glass for her second helping of bubbly.

"Fine, go ahead, Mel. Tell us all about the dark and stormy night."

"Now that is not my fault," Mel says to Lyric before turning back to me. "It sounds cliché, but it *was* a dark and stormy night, and that's an important part of the story."

Lyric grins back at her, slightly appeased now that she has a second drink and has successfully annoyed Mel. Her hands go up, a surrender complete with a smirk, and Mel takes this as her cue to continue, uninterrupted. There's a sisterly vibe between them and even though I'm part of it in a way, I feel jealousy bubbling up, thinking about how this sort of conversation and playful chatter never happens at the restaurant.

"Okay then. Like I said, it was a dark and stormy night. The kind of surprise summer storm that comes on strong and out of nowhere. This particular storm cut out some of the traffic lights and our group was over an hour late. No big deal. Luckily for them, it was a random Tuesday evening, and they were the last class of the night anyway. I could wait.

"It starts off like a typical bachelorette class with the photo ops and drinks prior," Mel says. She's in a zone now and obviously has the specific details and wording memorized from telling it so often. I'm on the edge of my seat; I love a good story.

"But then the drinks are hitting hard and I realize they'd been drinking the entire time they were stuck in traffic. Lit up by the time we got into the room.

"And I'm like, okay. Who am I to judge? We're only doing a few standard spins and pole struts. A peek-a-boo here and there." Still sitting, she spreads her knees for a quick peek-a-boo as if we're unfamiliar with the most basic of moves and needed a visual. "No one's in heels and we're not doing inversions," she continues, her knees back together, "so I'm not too alarmed by their impaired state of mind."

The story is for me, but I can't help but chance a glance towards Luke. As much as I love a confident man who takes charge, I also love one who knows when to let someone else shine. That's just what he's doing now as he's all in on the story with nothing but genuine interest, even though he probably knows it by heart, too.

He doesn't butt in, he doesn't busy himself with something else, and he doesn't have that look about him that some people get where you can tell they're not actually listening and are instead thinking about whatever comment they're about to say as a response to the speaker they're actively ignoring.

He must have felt my gaze on him, because seemingly out of nowhere, he turns and our eyes lock. I should be embarrassed, caught in the act of ogling my pole instructor after class, but Luke doesn't have that way about him. When he turned to find me staring at him, he didn't even flinch. As if he'd expected it all along, welcomed the lingering gaze before meeting it head-on. He licks his lips before giving me a knowing half smile.

"I'm assuming she's just part of the bridal party," Mel says, her eyes back on me seconds after I turned away from Luke, "and happens to kick ass on the pole. A natural, right? Then, when I'm off to one of the back side poles helping some of the other girls, she hops on the main pole, my pole, and suddenly her tits are out."

"Holy shit!" I say, thoroughly pulled out of my daydreams of Luke's lips on mine and now trying to picture the infamous Tits Out Bachelorette party instead. Not the tits necessarily, though I admit I do appreciate a good pair, but the scenario as a whole.

"What song was playing? Was *she* wearing heels? Nipple tassels? I need more details!" I say. I'm so close to the edge of my seat I'm practically doing a variation of a wall sit exercise, but it seems to be the right way to play it since Mel's smile is only getting bigger along with everyone else's.

Despite the easygoing persona I'm projecting, and my authentic interest in her story, this is the part of the job where things get tricky for me. The authentic version of me, Anna Laurier, would have been content to turn down the drinks, or at the very least sit on the outside of the conversation, just waiting for the moment when I could escape back to my apartment. I never go out for drinks after waiting tables. It's not that I don't like my coworkers. I do. I just, in general, am not a huge fan of people. They let you down in the long run, so the trick is to keep everything superficial and short-lived. Eliminate the scenario of a long-run, and you eliminate the inevitable let down.

So this person, this Jessica Brown version of me, is an aberration. Sure, I partially said yes to the drinks because Luke's super easy on the eyes and I felt on top of the world after the class. Still, *I* would have sipped silently for a few minutes before gulping my drink faster than a sorority sister at her first frat party, likely slipping on a discarded feather boa or stiletto as I awkwardly dashed out of the room once my plastic glass was drained. Me egging on people I've just met and constantly interjecting where I can? I'm only behaving this way because it's my job. I get the confidence and the motivation to do it by reminding myself of my fridge full of food and my bills paid on time and in full. The bulk of my paycheck is coming from *this* part of the job. The part where I pretend I'm not socially awkward, and I work my ass off to quickly form solid connections with everyone at the studio. I need to be on.

"Too bad we didn't have the cameras back then. It was a sight to see," Mel says, leaning back and relishing the final memories of that fateful evening.

I glance up at the ceiling and notice for the first time that there's a small device off in the corner. A camera.

"No thanks," Lyric says, placing her empty glass down on the table for a second time. "It's bad enough to hear it over and over again. If there was footage, I would never hear the end of it."

"There are cameras?" I ask. I can't tell if Calista was merely a shitty tour guide (she did miss a few things I've noticed now that I'm elbows deep in the job) or if this was intentional. But why would she intentionally not tell me about the cameras, especially given the reason I'm here?

"Yeah, throughout the studio, in every room but the bathrooms. They went up after Calista said—" Lyric stops midsentence once she catches sight of Luke. His calm, laid-back demeanor is gone and in its place is a glare of sorts.

Mel busies herself with her drink, first taking a giant gulp and then feigning unwavering interest in the structure of the cheap plastic glass. Real subtle.

"I installed all the security cameras a few months back," Luke says. He sets his half-empty glass down and I wonder if that's the end of his after-work drinking, because he's all business now. "It's mostly to protect us. We're an inclusive studio; we have people of all genders attending and teaching the classes, classes that sometimes include performing provocative moves in skimpy clothing, or performing semi-dangerous moves with slippery, sweaty hands. Sometimes there's alcohol involved." He motions towards the bottle of champagne that was supposed to have been drunk during the bachelorette session.

I nod my head in understanding, but I must still look a little confused. I shouldn't have had that drink on an empty stomach. It's messing with my ability to shield my thoughts and emotions. Jessica Brown's reaction should be bubbly indifference, but I'm having trouble channeling it.

"Did Calista not mention it to you?" he asks. "When we're setting up our first lessons, we reach out a few times to our incoming students about expectations, and we always mention the cameras. We don't want to catch anyone off-guard."

Like when he unexpectedly came into the studio and I almost destroyed my knees? Sure, I can understand that. Surprises in this line of work are not good.

I take a quick superficial reading of the room and assume it's okay to give a slight dig towards the boss. I need to gauge where everyone stands with Calista. Is there really a divide like she claims there is?

"No, she didn't." I pause for a beat or two before casually adding, "Is that typical for her? To forget or overlook things?" I raise my voice at the end, beyond what's necessary for a question, and I swirl around what's left of my drink. The epitome of casual.

Or so I thought. The comment falls overwhelmingly short, or I'm on the right track and everyone's scared to say anything. Lyric and Mel hop up and start talking about how they have a long day tomorrow or animals and children at home to get back to. They gather things, they throw out their cups, and then they're out the door with calls of "See you tomorrow" as the door shuts and locks behind them.

"I should get going, too," Luke says as he clears the bottle and his cup from the table. And even though I just witnessed it all with my own eyes, I'm second-guessing what exactly it was that I saw, or thought I saw. Because Luke's demeanor is back to normal, and I don't really know Lyric and Mel beyond our quick drink. Maybe they're like that–one minute they're more laid back than Cheech and Chong, and the next minute they remember they're adults with responsibilities they need to get back to.

With genuine concern and a softness in his voice, Luke says, "Looks like you'll have a bit of a bruise on your knees there." He points to my knees, which are indeed turning an angry shade of red. My skin is naturally pale, so he's right. Those bad boys will be a glorious collage of purple, blue, and green in no time.

"Probably, but bruises come with the job," I say as he helps me up from the couch. How in the hell did that happen? I'm older but I'm not geriatric; I do not need help standing up from a couch. And yet, as if it was second nature, he extended his hand, and I took it.

"Pole kisses," he says, still holding my hand in his. His head is tilted down towards mine because he has a slight height advantage, and our lips are inches away from each other. At the word "kisses" I see his eyes instinctively lock in on my lips and I'm wondering if he's thinking about kissing me or if the word itself caused the connection and made his eyes, against his will, focus in on the body part that's involved with that particular activity.

I don't wait to find out the answer. I let go of his hand to pick up my bag, then we're back to small talk as we head out of the studio. Like the gentleman I'm pretty sure he is, he holds the door for me and we're again in extremely close proximity. A tingling sensation rushes through my body as I break out in goosebumps, and I know for certain it's not from the cooler night air. It's him, and the gestures of offering me a hand on the couch and holding the door open for me felt purposeful. Because that door could have been opened a foot wider, but then my body wouldn't have been practically against his when we left. And his half smile after the word kiss, as if it were an invitation for me to close what little space remained between us. Not to mention the countless times our eyes met during class and I could practically feel the heat coming from his gaze. I thought we had a moment in the coffee shop, and everything since then has only confirmed those suspicions.

"You were great tonight, with Ellen," he says. His walk is casual. Almost a strut with what appears to be some sort of never-ending natural confidence, but also purposeful and thoughtful as he immediately takes his place on the outside of the sidewalk.

"She was fun. I enjoy a good, forceful personality."

He nods appreciatively. I imagine he's seen a variety of large personalities going through the studio. Has seen it all, likely.

"What about you? How did you learn to…" I don't know how to word it just yet, and we continue to walk a few more steps while I sort it out in my head. "You create a sense of calm. Even your voice, it's different during class than outside of it. Your mannerisms." I don't find the words I'm looking for, so I let the wrong ones out and hope for the best. "You're pretty cocky outside of class, but as an instructor, you'd never know."

He laughs at that, just like he laughed at the coffee shop. "Yeah, it's a fair assessment to say I'm confident. I have good reason to be. But in the studio, it can be intimidating and is rarely helpful. Especially in a 101 class. I treat that almost like

I'm an actor taking on the role of a patient, not cocky instructor. You know what I mean?"

If I didn't know any better, I would swear he was looking into my soul and waiting patiently for my confession about how I know exactly what he means because I am doing the same, as we speak.

"Yeah, I think I do," I say, dropping the topic and hoping he does the same.

As he walks down the block with me, both of us heading back towards that coffee shop where this all began, he keeps throwing me this cocky half-smile sort of smirk that I can't even be mad about because I know I'm sending all the wrong signals back. But I can't let this happen. When his hand brushes the back of mine, I take a casual step to the side to avoid an "accidental" recurrence. His smile is too wicked and those eyes are full of heat and promises of what could be if I'd only let nature take its course.

Nope, nope, nope.

Now, if we were at the restaurant and he was at one of my tables and said he was only in town for the night? Absolutely. Let's do this thing. Age ain't nothing but a number. But a coworker at the job where I'm supposed to be spying on the employees? That's a terrible idea. An idea that's so bad it could cost me thousands of dollars. I have no doubt that sex with Luke would be absolutely earth shattering. I've seen the man move, and if he can actually fuck me with half of the intensity he's throwing at me while he's eye fucking me right now, I don't know that one time would even be enough to satisfy me.

"Which station are you?" he says as we come up to the corner of W. 41st and 8th. "We already passed my station, but I want to make sure you get on safely. I'll ride with you to your apartment if you'd like. Late night subway rides are always interesting."

Yes, there's mischief in his eyes, but I get the feeling it's also coming from kindness. It's late and I'm a woman walking alone at night. Still, I'm feeling confident with my bedazzled pepper spray in my purse, and I really don't think my will-power is going to last if I temp this any further.

"I'm right up here. Thank you for offering to ride with me. Very generous, but I've got Ol' Bessy to handle any nonsense," I say, holding up my sparkling seasoning weapon, "so I think I'll be okay."

"Okay then." His expression shows mild disappointment with a hint of intrigue at Ol' Bessy. "I'll see you at your next class then."

The man is undeterred. I bet he's one of those types that likes a good chase. Poor guy. He has no idea he can chase me all he wants, but my current obsession with this studio is unwavering. I have work to do and nothing can impede that.

CHAPTER 6
LUKE, WEDNESDAY, JULY 3RD

'm at the front desk with Florence shooting the shit and waiting for Jessi's class to end so I can ambush her with a quick, impromptu photo shoot. It's been over a year since we've added a new instructor photo to the wall–hence my initial hesitation when Calista quickly hired Jessi when I hadn't even known she was looking for an additional instructor. Now that I've seen her in action, I'm eager to do what I can to help make sure she's in it for the long haul. Besides, it's about time we got some fresh blood in here.

"What did she study in Juilliard?" Florence asks.

"Dance?" I answer. I've never met anyone that went there and don't know what specific majors or programs they offer.

Florence throws me a *are you a fucking moron* look. "What *kind* of dance?"

"I don't know. Dance. Why are you asking?"

"No reason." She picks up the nail polish bottle and gives it a shake before starting on her second coat. Florence goes through spurts of business at the front desk. The number and needs of customers and clients ebb and flow, sometimes arbitrarily. Since when it's dead, it's really dead, she keeps a myriad of supplies at the desk to keep herself occupied. One year she learned to crochet and for Christmas everyone got a pair of leg warmers in the colors of our studio: black and hot pink. My roommate Trav thoroughly enjoys my pair. Now, according to Mel, Florence has some top secret project on her computer. Nothing she's ready to share yet, but I'm hoping she's secretly revamping the website and learning all the tech things so I can finally be relieved of that part of the job.

Calista went through college with dial-up internet and the very beginnings of Facebook. I still remember her saying random things about people writing on her wall. Since my college experience was vastly more tech advanced than hers, I was her go-to for all her tech help, even before I officially worked for her. I'm ready to be done with that part of it now.

"I'm curious about my coworkers," she says. "Aren't you?"

I shrug. Trying not to reveal too soon that I do, in fact, want to know every little thing about Jessi. Are her parents like mine? Kind, but mostly aloof? Was she like me as a kid? Outgoing and determined to be the class clown, consequences be damned? What would her ideal weekend be and how would I play a leading role in that weekend? What makes her laugh? If she was on a deserted island with one movie and one CD, would it also be *Dazed and Confused* and Tom Petty's greatest hits? Does she listen to sad music when she's sad, and if so, which song is her go-to?

"You're a terrible liar, Luke. No offense intended. As someone who's endured multiple lying, cheating husbands, I find it endearing and down-right sexy how inept you are at it. But I think you should know it's not your strong point, sweetie."

"Thanks?"

Florence goes back to her nails while I fiddle with the camera settings on my phone. I haven't done one of these in a while and I'm trying to remember the filters I used to capture the perfect black and white action photo. One of the biggest appeals of the wall of photos is that they all look uniform. I also feel slight pressure to not fuck it up because Calista approved me to order an extra framed photo to give to instructors to put up on their own walls at home. I don't want to give Jessi something unworthy of her walls; I don't want her to equate crap with me.

"She's closed off. You know?" Florence asks, as if we're still in the middle of the conversation, even though no one's spoken for quite a while. "She'll ask me a bunch of questions, but if I ask her something, she gives some one-word response before scurrying off. Always in a hurry, that one."

I shrug to keep up my pretense of indifference. I may be a terrible liar, but that won't stop me from trying. My mother practically nicknamed me Persistent Little Fucker when I was in middle school.

"What questions did you ask?" I can't help it. Jessi crosses my mind more than she should, and I'm starved to talk to someone about her. Not my roommates; someone who knows her.

"Today I asked her where she lives and she said Sunny-side. When I asked her about whatever town she lived in in Pennsylvania—I can't remember the name of it—she gave me some generic summary of a blue house and picket white fence before blowing me off and saying she had to get ready for her next class. It wasn't even starting for another twenty minutes. None of the students were here yet."

She puts the cap back on her nail polish, carefully lays her hands palms down on the desk, and turns her attention to me.

Jessi seemed pretty open to me at the coffee shop and during and after class, but I don't think that's what Florence wants to hear.

"Maybe she's a private person."

We're the only ones at the desk, and the only ones in the building who aren't currently in one of the studios for a class.

She leans over and whispers conspiratorially, anyway. "Jessi lies to baristas when they ask for her name. She gives them a fake one because she doesn't want them calling out her real name in front of a bunch of strangers."

I knew it! I could have sworn her name was Anna at the coffee shop, but I was so focused on not making an ass out of myself, I wasn't really paying that close attention to other stuff happening around me. When I got to class and she was Jessi to everyone, I assumed I had just misheard or misremembered.

"I played along saying that was smart because there are all kinds of dangerous people out there, but I don't think that's why she did it. I think she's in the witness protection program."

Florence is dead serious, and I don't have any proof or reason to believe otherwise. Well, aside from the obvious that it's highly unlikely Jessi was involved in something so sinister and dangerous it required her to uproot her old life for an entirely new one.

"Yeah, maybe," I concede, mostly to humor her.

"I searched social media for her and can't find anything. What thirty-something year old woman doesn't have a Facebook account?"

I shrug. Aside from the instructors at the studio and a handful of Calista's friends, most of my friends are in their twenties.

"You're taking her picture? The same picture you're going to put on the website?"

I nod.

"Interesting. Let me know how that goes." She gives me an exaggerated wink and starts blowing on her bright purple nails.

· · ·

Florence's witness protection theory is quickly put to rest when Jessi's students file out of the room and I slip in.

"How was class?" I ask as a formality. Anyone with eyes could see it went well. Jessi's face is flushed, but in a good way. There's a glow about her and that trademark smile that absolutely kills me. I've had plenty of women smile at me, but Jessi's is my all-time favorite. Yes, it's a beautiful smile, but it's the personality that comes out through it that gets me every time. In the few days since we met, Jessi's started to throw this crazy, from the soul, look at me that melts my insides.

This is the smile she gives me now. Like she didn't think things could get any better, but then she saw me and she was genuinely so happy for the positive addition to her day.

"I nailed it, naturally," she says as she seemingly floats around the room, tossing stray rags into the bin and grabbing a clean one to wipe down the poles. "I thought you had off today."

I stifle a smile that comes from her knowing my schedule, though I'm sure she can read it on my face.

"I am, but I had a bit of free time and figured this would be the best opportunity to get some work orientation stuff out of the way."

She's regarding me with her hands on her hips, an eyebrow cocked.

"Jessi Brown, you've officially made it through multiple days of pole instruction without running for the door *and* without losing a single student. Therefore, you have earned your position on the highly coveted Wall of Instructors."

Jessi's grin increases tenfold before her hands are over her mouth. "Really?" she asks, slightly muffled by her fingers.

"Really," I say, nodding and holding up my phone. "Is now a good time?"

She fusses with her hair and glances down at her outfit. "I kinda look like a bum with my hair in a messy ponytail."

Because I don't want to completely scare her off, I don't tell her that's impossible, and she's the most gorgeous woman I've ever seen. Instead, I shake my head and say, "Not a bum. You look authentic."

"Okay. If you're sure." She fixes her ponytail, and it falls exactly as it did a few moments prior, though she doesn't seem to notice.

"I'm sure. I've taken all the pictures hanging on the wall; look at them again and you'll notice the imperfections."

"Oh, I will. Let me grab my water bottle and phone—"

"No need. We're good in this room. I just need to make a few minor adjustments to the lighting." I do that on my phone. I balked at first when Calista insisted we have wall *and* phone access to the lights in the studios, but I admit I've been relying on my phone as a remote control far more than I ever thought I would.

Jessi stands in the center of the room, watching me while fidgeting with her fingers. Which is funny because in my mind, if anyone's going to be nervous here, it should be me. I haven't done this in over a year; I had to YouTube a few how-to videos to relearn how to replicate the photos on the wall. And now I'm fumbling with the F and ISO settings on my phone, and the more I feel her eyes on me, the more my giant thumbs fuck up the delicate settings I'm going for.

"How about some music?" I say, for both our sakes. "Your choice."

Jessi jumps at the suggestion. "I have the perfect summer playlist." Lana Del Rey's "Doin' Time" spills out from the speakers and the tension in the room slowly dissolves like waves retreating into the ocean.

"Am I actually dancing or just posing on the pole?" she asks, already up and doing a back hook spin. She uses her free hand to pull out her hair band, letting her long brown locks almost dust the floor as she turns.

"Today, we're going to master the art of posing while looking like you're not posing."

Her momentum stops and she's facing away from me, but she turns her head to look back over her shoulder, and I take my first shot.

"Perfect. Now ease your left shoulder down." Just like in class, I don't touch her to help move her into position. Instructors never touch; verbal directions only. "Yeah, right there. And look forward, then back at me. That's it. Nice and slow."

We transition to other positions, taking breaks in-between because I'm asking her to hold poses on the pole after she just did two back-to-back classes. I maybe could have waited for a better time to do this, but to be honest, I've already held back by waiting until today.

While we're "working," I casually ask her a few questions and take entirely too many pictures in the process.

"You're from Pennsylvania, right?"

I can't tell if I'm imagining it or not, but I could have sworn I saw the slightest twitch in her expression. I make a mental note to potentially back off of family stuff. I can relate with an older sister who's drifting farther away from me by the day, and two parents who obviously didn't want kids the first time around, and really didn't want the second oops baby over a decade after the first.

"Yeah, Doylestown. It's a suburb outside of Philly," she says, using the tone of someone who's said this a million times when anyone asks where she's from. Looks like Florence was over-reaching again. I need to stop letting her get into my head. I also need to stop projecting my shitty childhood on everyone else.

"Did you like it there?" Suburban people fascinate me, just like when I meet someone who tells me they were home-schooled and I can't wrap my mind around how they weren't surrounded by millions of strangers at all times while they were growing up.

She shrugs as much as someone can while they're gripping the pole and hanging on for dear life. "It was okay. A little too uppity for me sometimes."

I nod like I know exactly how uppity Doylestown residents can be and I couldn't agree more with her assessment.

"Wait, that's perfect. Don't move a muscle."

She's doing somewhat simple moves, mostly what you'd see in a beginner's class, but they photograph well. Especially the albatross, which is what she's doing now. She's halfway up the pole with one leg hooked and holding her weight, while the other extends out to the left, perfectly perpendicular to the pole. Her torso is leaning forward like she's coming right at me, and one hand is on her extended leg, while the other is held out to the other side. At first glance, you'd think she was flying.

"Okay," I say after I've taken a few shots. "Now move your right arm–"

"Touch me, Luke," Jessi practically begs, and I know I'll hear her voice saying those three words over and over in my head at random times throughout the day for the foreseeable future. "Just move my body wherever it needs to go. Please."

"Right. I'll uh..." I say before giving up on words and focusing on her request.

I clear my throat as one hand tentatively cups her elbow. She's tense on the pole, but loosens up any part I'm working with and her arm easily moves up the few centimeters I need it to so that it lines up perfectly with her extended leg. Unable to resist, I let my fingers graze her forearm when I move down to her hand. As I maneuver each finger, I marvel at the contrast of the soft, smooth skin on the back of her hand versus the slightly rough, callused skin on her palm.

"Luke," she says in a husky voice that has my cock's full

attention. "I've been holding this pose for a while now. Can you hurry up and take the picture?"

Oh, right. Not a husky voice. It's the voice of someone straining with physical exertion. Even so, the goosebumps covering her body tell me she's feeling something, too. The photoshoot might be over–this shot is the one, I can tell–but Jessi and I are just beginning. The one good thing about Calista drifting away? I don't feel quite as beholden to her "don't sleep with the coworkers" golden rule.

CHAPTER 7
ANNA, MONDAY, JULY 8TH

pause in the middle of my living room arts and crafts project when I hear my phone ding and see a new message from Calista. She checked in via text already, right after my first two days, to make sure everything was going well. There was a motherly feel to her messages. And while we kept to the business at hand, the conversations were friendly enough. You'd never know thousands were at stake, that her business and financial security were at stake.

This conversation is different.

Have you found anything?

No hello; no question about how I'm doing. Straight to the point. It's a reminder that while Calista and Paige are friends, Calista and I are not. We are strictly employer and employee, no matter how comfortable we got with each other during my initial training.

Nothing yet

I immediately regret the text as soon as it pops up on the

screen. That is not what Calista wants to hear. It's too blunt and careless. It looks apathetic there on the screen beneath her inquiry. I start typing so she knows there's more coming; I'll figure it out as I go.

> I've been trying to hang out by the desk before and between classes. Florence is careful about what screens are up. Just the home screen when she's not actively using it

I exhale. That looks better, but I should add more.

> I'll keep working on it. She's an open book but I can't tell if she's careful about the computer for your benefit or her own.

I keep going while Calista gives the occasional reactions (thumbs up, heart, exclamation marks) to my text bubbles. It's only been a little over a week since I've started in the studio, but I surprise myself with how active I've been as I list out what I've noticed about different employees and the methods I've used to go out of my way to interact with them: brunch with Lux and Grace, the two instructors who run the booty sculpting and chair dancing classes; the photoshoot with Luke; doing an open studio session with Mel and Lyric.

For just over a week, it looks good. It looks like I've earned my initial payment and am on my way to get the final installment. Sure, I don't have anything to report yet, but I'm confident I'm showing initiative.

As I wait for Calista to send something back that's not a reaction, I fend off the gnawing feeling in my gut that's surfaced at least once a day since this whole thing started: What if I'm chasing after nothing?

It's possible. My father was paranoid about things. The most glaring moment that replays in my memory in vivid fashion is the time my mother said something about leaving her coat at home next time, but my father, with his poor hearing, turned it into "let's leave Dad home next time." He was so pissed and no one could convince him that wasn't what she said.

Calista could be suffering from the same affliction: mishearing what others are saying and thinking the worst. Seeing things that aren't there and then building them up in her head to be the ultimate betrayal when it's actually nothing.

My phone buzzes, but when I pull up my screen, it's a message from Luke. Despite the stress that's tearing up my stomach, I slide down into my couch, my muscles relaxing. Luke has that effect on me already.

> I need to ask you a serious question.
> Remember, there is no right or wrong answer.
> Just your opinion.

As soon as I finish reading, an image pops up on the screen. It's Luke, holding up a pair of tiny shorts on a hanger next to his head. His expression reads a cross between nervous and eager. His glasses are slightly cocked, like maybe he knocked them with the hanger but didn't notice.

Calista picks now to finally respond in great detail about how I shouldn't get *too* close to anyone, but she wants me to carry on with what I'm already doing. I wonder how she'd feel about Luke sending me a picture of what looked like a supermodel's pair of boy shorts panties.

> Remember the end goal is for you to find the thief, me to fire them, then I go back to business as usual with no one knowing.

> The staff can't know the real reason you were there

> Don't get too close. Find a balance

What a coincidence she would tell me this just as Luke is once again throwing me beyond off balance. My time around him reminds me of being on a see-saw as a child. Feet flat on the sturdy ground one minute, and the next, I'm up in the air with this pleasant and exciting feeling of my stomach flip-flopping from the sudden skyrocketing motion towards the sun.

> I understand. I've got this.

I switch the messages back to Luke. To the random onlooker, his pictures would appear inappropriate, or at the very least, unprofessional. But we've actually talked about it before in the studio. At the end of the month, Luke is competing in a pole competition at a bar not too far from our studio. Aside from the accolades that would surely come from winning a local bar pole competition, what he's really trying to do is get the word out about the studio and drum up some more clients. So while the picture at first glance looks to be a bit forward for a message between coworkers, it's on target given the context. Still, I have to ignore the feeling that this is too close and not the balance Calista was preaching about.

I mentally push Calista out of the equation and tap Luke's picture so that it now takes up the entire screen. His youth comes through in his unabashed smile. Another reminder that he is way too young. He probably wants kids in ten years or so, which will be when I'm over 50.

With all of these reminders of why I should not engage in playful banter with this alluring man, one would think I'd do the right thing and diffuse whatever sexual tension continues to build between us.

Too bad the right thing is rarely the enticing option. Besides, just because we're flirting doesn't mean we have to have sex.

I hold up my phone to send an equally silly image back where my eyes are bulging.

> So that's a no? Too risqué for a pole competition?

I smile at the total nerd he is for using an accent in his text.

> You said there was no wrong answer

> No one ever means that. I already bought them. Non-refundable.

> Look again. Take your time before you answer

He sends another photo. This time, in place of his unabashed grin, is a pout. His head is cocked slightly to the side and his eyes are looking towards those same itty bitty shorts.

I do take my time before I answer, and then over the course of an hour, we accomplish a lot together. The itty bitty shorts debate is settled with Luke definitely wearing them for the competition. He doesn't tell which song he's using (I think he still doesn't know) but he does send me a few short videos of a few moves and asks for my opinion on each.

At this, I feel torn and mildly guilty. Luke is asking about pole moves and dancing advice, believing that I am Juilliard graduate Jessica Brown. Would he even bother if he knew it was plain old Anna Laurier? Would he hold *my* opinion to such esteem that he would consider making changes to his routine? No, I don't think he would.

CHAPTER 8
CALISTA, WEDNESDAY, JULY 10TH

'm in bed. Again. I don't have debilitating pain anywhere in my body, but I also can't find the motivation to get up. Any time I send out whatever brain signals are in charge of moving limbs, I'm met with the overwhelming feeling that each arm and leg weigh at least 20 pounds. It's mentally painful how exhausting being alive is right now.

I stop trying to get up.

I sleep a lot.

I doom scroll on my phone.

I DoorDash Chinese food.

I run the studio through text messages with the staff.

"Cally!" I hear Roderick call from the main living space. I blame Herman, my doorman with a heart of gold, for letting it slip that I'm home. Rod's too charming; even if Herman insisted no one was allowed up to see me, Rod would find a way to convince him otherwise.

"Cal," he says again, gently opening my bedroom door and peeking in, as if afraid of what he might see.

"What?" I ask. And I mean it. What else is there to say? He hasn't called or texted in well over a month. It's actually been such a relief without him here. Some days, I drink wine and gobble down edibles as soon as I wake up. Some days I scream into my pillow before collapsing into gut-wrenching sobs. I couldn't do that when he was around. Always there, always watching me as if I could break at any minute.

"Jesus, Cal," he says, ignoring that no one actually invited him into my room or into my condo, for that matter.

He goes over to the windows, the ones that look out to the balcony and the city beyond, and wrestles them open. I immediately feel the breeze and the hit of fresh air. It's soothing and welcome, but Rod is not. Can't I wallow in peace?

"Leave me alone," I say with little conviction.

"You can't live like this." He's tossing dirty clothes into the laundry basket. Not sure who he thinks is going to wash them.

"I have been. It's fine."

He looks like he's contemplating sitting on the bed to talk, but then thinks better of it. I don't blame him. I don't know the last time I washed my bed sheets or even the last time I washed my hair.

"You're not fine."

"I'm not your concern."

"This isn't healthy," he says, ignoring my blatant invitation for him to leave my life forever. Just like he did back in May.

"Please go away." I haven't moved since he showed up. I'm still in bed, curled up in the fetal position with *ER* streaming in the background. There's a comfort in rewatching a show from my early childhood. A time before things became so complicated that getting up to brush my teeth feels like too much. I simply cannot be bothered with it.

"When's the last time you were at the studio?" he asks.

I roll my eyes. It's like we never broke up.

I haven't been to the studio since I finished training Anna to take over my class. I immediately transitioned from three intense weeks of pole training her during the days and instructing my classes at night, to this bedroom.

It's my fault I'm so low right now. I took months' worth of energy and mental capacity and used it all up over the course of three weeks. Now I wait here, patiently, until I recharge. Or not. Maybe I don't rebound. I'm starting to not care one way or the other.

"Come on, Cally. Say something. I'm sorry things didn't work out between us, but you're not going to throw your life away over it, are you?"

There it is. He thinks this is about him. I'm curled up in a ball, wasting away because the handsome and charismatic Roderick Miller broke my heart.

"Leave," I say, not wanting to get into how this has nothing to do with him. I don't care what he thinks anymore, and I don't have the energy to argue.

It takes almost an hour of him saying things and me mostly ignoring him, but Rod does eventually leave with his jacket and signed *Star Wars* poster, the real reason he stopped by in the first place. I remind myself that he wasn't grilling me out of romantic concern; he did it because I looked like death and he felt obligated. My relationship with Rod is officially over.

I can't help but wonder if I can say the same about instructing pole. Are pole and I officially over as well? I wince just thinking about it. I have two perfectly good poles one floor above me, going to waste. The same could be said about the studio.

There's a clear memory of me playing tag as a small child at one of the local playgrounds. I was there with a nanny; no way would Mom or Dad drop their work and social life to take me. After my game, I sat on one of the park benches with my nanny, hoping that more kids would show up to play. We chatted while I waited and at one point I told her how sad I was for her since she was all grown up and couldn't play anymore. I can't recall her name, but I do remember how she explained that when people get older, their interests change. They change. It sounded preposterous at the time. Who would ever tire of playing games?

It's me. I tired of playing games, and now I'm tired of pole and running the studio. It's felt like a chore for over a year now, where I'm pushing myself to do this thing that hurts me and zaps what little energy I have. Why?

When I can't come up with a decent answer to my own question, I take a deep breath and pull up my email on my phone. There's one from my next-door neighbor from over a year ago. She offered to buy me out so she can expand her budding condo empire in the building. It was a staggering amount thanks to the booming real estate market, but still not enough to make me consider such a thing. I was living my best life in New York, with a fabulous two-story condo, walking distance from my studio.

But now? I've been opening and rereading that email. The first time was with Paige. We were drunk at the condo waiting for Anna's shift to end, and Paige joked about how if it were her condo, she would sell the place and travel the world, because surely I could make a fortune if I ever put it on the market. She shrieked when I showed her the email, and she understood when I said I would never.

Was that really only last month? How quickly things change.

Next, I pull up the security cameras from the studio. Some days I can watch the studio function flawlessly without me, feeling nothing but happiness for the people who can still instruct without feeling like they're dying for the next few days. Today feels like one of those days, so I watch for a while, feeling more detached by the minute. They don't need me anymore.

I switch over from Lux's class to Anna's. This whole Anna experiment, along with me being MIA from the studio, it's been eye-opening to say the least. I don't know what I expected from the Anna arrangement. In hindsight, I think it was more about finding and fixing a problem that's actually fixable. I can't do much about my traitorous body and mind, but a traitorous employee? That I have the power to control. I was so eager for her to find something, for me to swoop in and do whatever needed to be done, but then what?

I hadn't thought it through beyond that. I also hadn't considered that maybe it was always me. There is some underhanded activity, sure. That I know almost for certain. But it's not enough to make the financial dent that I'm telling Paige and Anna about. Now that I've taken a few giant steps away from the business, I can see that the money is running out because I'm a mediocre business manager who refused to hire an accountant.

Like an absolute maniac, the epiphany makes me throw back my head and laugh. Fuck, I haven't laughed in weeks. But the idea that I'm losing everything and imploding my dream life is somehow inexplicably funny to me.

My phone vibrates with a text from Lyric. She wants permission to order a giant cardboard cut-out of Luke wearing his contest costume of a tiny pair of black shorts.

Luke would abhor having that at the studio, and that's reason enough for me to approve it. *He needs to lighten up a little*, I think as I unwrap my first edible of the day.

CHAPTER 9
ANNA, FRIDAY, JULY 12TH

"Holy shit…" Paige says, standing in front of the black wall in my apartment. I hand her a glass of wine, which she absently accepts but doesn't drink.

I have to admit that any other reaction from her would have been disappointing. There was a time when I was younger, in grade school, when I was torn about what I wanted to be when I grew up: an actor, a dancer, or an artist. My lack of artistic ability narrowed those choices down for me, but it never killed my desire to create beauty any way that I can.

For almost as long as I've lived here, I've kept this one five-foot section of apartment wall completely bare of any paint, shelves, and pictures. I didn't have much wall space to begin with, so the quarantined five-foot section has been kind of a big deal, especially since I've done jack shit with it so far.

Not anymore. Not only did I finally do something with it, but I went beyond bold by painting it with chalkboard paint and then decorating it with colored chalk to write out all the upcoming classes happening the rest of July and all of August. Fancy handwriting, little doodles, color-coordinated classes–it really is a work of art. Just as Paige is standing before it with an untouched wine glass, zero words as she looks over every detail, I've done the same at least a half dozen times since its creation on Monday.

"This is…" she says, taking a few steps back until she's leaning against the arm of the love seat. Unable to find the right words, she settles instead for some wine.

"I know. It really is," I agree, but I stop there. It's not like she needs to know I once turned my couch so that instead of facing my TV, I was facing the wall for a good hour. Just taking it all in and mentally planning out my month. As an instructor, I get to join in on any of the classes for free as long as there's room, and during studio hours I have access to the poles for open studio sessions as long as there aren't any classes scheduled.

It broke Diesel's heart when I called to cut down my shifts by half, especially during the summer, but I told him it was only temporary. Not sure if that was a lie or not. I'm hoping that it was and there's some sort of weird alternate reality where this position as Jessica Brown isn't just a four-week temporary spy gig.

Regardless, in the meantime, I want to fill my days with pole work, whether that means I'm doing targeted practice to finally build up to inversions, or taking on instructing additional lower-level classes now that I've proved myself with my current success in Calista's Pole 101 class.

"It's July 12th. Why aren't you at–does that really say Karaoke Pole? People are swinging and singing as we speak?" Paige's voice is full of deep admiration. Not only can Paige not dance, even if her life depended on it, her voice can shatter windows. The combination of the two lacking skills destroyed her early childhood dreams of becoming a Broadway star. We frequently bonded over our shared shattered dreams when we first met ages ago.

"Yup," I say, double-checking the time on my phone since

I didn't realize it was already after eight. "Some more successfully than others, I'm sure."

"But not you? Not in the singing mood tonight?"

I shake my head. "Not tonight. As much as I've been fully immersing myself in all of this, my body is screaming for a break."

Paige glares at me.

"Fine. I'm annoyed with the person running the class." I don't have a tell. I'm certain of it, but sometimes Paige has magical powers when it comes to me lying. This must be one of those times. I'm not even sure why I lied in the first place. If anything, she's going to be completely on board with the rant I'm about to spew.

"Let it out, Anna. I'm always here for it," she says before taking a generous pull from her glass.

"Sonya runs the karaoke classes; she's… too much."

"There you go. Now give me the details," Paige encourages. Having gotten her fill of my pole studio calendar, she vacates her position against the couch arm and moves over to an actual seat on a cushion so we can settle in. She can tell this one might get messy.

"She always comes into the studio with the biggest smile–blindingly white teeth flashing everywhere. Asking anyone she encounters how they're doing, how their family is, and something specific about them, like she's being quizzed on how well she was listening to whatever conversation she last had with them." I hitch my voice up an octave or two for my imitation of Sonya: "How's your husband's hernia? Is your pup feeling better? I picked this flower for you on the way in because it's bright and sunny, just like your soul."

I end my rant by pretending to gag as I mock retch off the side of the couch.

"That fucking bitch," Paige deadpans, a fake look of menace in her narrowed eyes. "Want me to Tanya Harding her and take a bat to her knees for you? Sounds like I'd be doing the entire studio a favor."

"Stop," I say through a light laugh. "I know. I sound like a psychopath right now, but you don't understand. That explosion of pep isn't natural. It's like talking to a pod person. I can't be in her classes. I'll just be pissed off the whole time and then I'll be labeled the bitch."

"The bitch who hates the nicest person in the world," she says, clarifying what I was skirting around because it all sounds so petty when it's said aloud.

"I don't hate the nicest person in the world. I hate the coked-up, female version of Mr. Rogers. There's a big difference. Also, she asks a million questions about me and I'm trying to keep the details of my personal life low-key."

Irritated from talking about Sonya, I look down at the coffee table to grab some comfort food, only to realize I haven't put anything out. What I have in the cabinet I use as a pantry won't be nearly as fancy as Calista's spread, but Paige would never expect anything like that. Besides, if I keep up what I'm doing now, maybe one day I'll be running one of Calista's studios and earning enough to eat like a queen now and then.

"Let me grab some stuff to snack on while we're talking," I say, hopping up from the couch to make the quick trip to the kitchen, which is actually just a small corner of my apartment. No shouting needed. We're within earshot at all times in this tiny living space.

"Before I forget," Paige says, "I texted you a link earlier. Did you get it?"

"No, I don't think so." I pick up my phone and check anyway. I have this habit of seeing texts and then thinking I'll remember to respond to them later, and then immediately forgetting. "Yeah, nothing here." I toss my phone back on the couch and walk into the kitchen.

"Huh. Weird. I'll send it again. Just a pole article I thought you'd like."

"Please do. I'm obsessed."

From the kitchen I hear my phone make a soft vibrating confirmation that it got the article.

"Okay. Sent. So, have you reported anything back to Calista yet?" Paige asks while I'm rooting around my make-shift pantry. "I love working from home, but I miss all the gossip that comes from working face-to-face with people. I'll have to live vicariously through you now that you're going to have actual dirt at the studio. Your pizza palace gossip hasn't been cutting it."

"Unfortunately, no. Nothing worth mentioning, yet." Calista sent yet another text yesterday asking for an update. And while she was once again really nice, even though I had absolutely nothing for her, I'm worried that she's growing impatient. Makes sense. Time is ticking. If she's having financial issues with the studio, time could easily mean money. Lots of money, depending on her circumstances.

At the reminder, I feel even more guilty for taking the night off, and vow for the third time this week to get my shit together and focus more on the spying part and less on the pole dancing aspect of the job. It's just so hard when one is clearly much more rewarding and enjoyable than the other.

"That's a bummer," Paige says, unconcerned. "Any hot guys?"

My hand pauses as my mind races. Did I mention Luke before? I don't think so, but my lips get loose around Paige, especially when wine is involved.

"At a pole dancing studio? Not likely. It's 90% women," I say, grabbing the first bag of crunchy snacks my hand lands on. Time to get back to the living room.

She's scrolling through my phone when I get to the couch with my sorry-looking, half-empty bag of cheesy cracker bites. Not that either of us is paying attention to the food.

"Give me that," I say, snatching the phone from her hand. She's scrolling through a text message thread between me and Luke. There's a new one from him, likely what I heard when I was in the kitchen; there isn't an article from Paige. That freaking ninja. She got me to unlock my phone right before leaving the room.

"You owe me a superb article on pole dancing. It better blow my fucking mind it's so good."

"That's probably not going to happen. Now, tell me all about you and Calista's little brother. Emphasis on little. I remember taking him out for ice cream when Calista's family visited her at college. What a cutie pie. Loved to get extra whipped cream on everything. Or maybe you already know about his affinity for licking whipped cream off his desserts?"

I don't react. I don't know how to react to this. Luke is Calista's brother? *And* he's not just a baby-faced thirty-something year old? He's actually that young?

"Calm down," Paige says, accurately assessing my lack of a reaction as a sort of catatonic freak-out. "It's not like you haven't been with younger guys before."

"I haven't *been* with Luke," I retort, not bothering to touch the whole age thing since she knows all the dirt about my one-night stands. "And I had no idea he's Calista's brother. Neither of them said anything."

"You haven't been with him *yet*, maybe, but those texts are borderline an HR nightmare."

I scroll back through to double-check. How does she even know? I was in the kitchen for all of a minute, if that.

"I'm a quick reader," she adds while I scroll. "Calista said she didn't want you knowing too much going into it. Maybe that's why she didn't tell you. Keep you unbiased."

"Maybe," I concede. And I could see why Luke wouldn't say anything if he's trying to get out from under his older sister. Damn. I can't even be mad at the withholding of information given that I'm flat out lying to people about who I am.

Luke and I have been texting for the past week and a half. Ever since the photo shoot. It started out work-related. Luke sent out a group text inviting everyone to Pole Masters, the pole dancing competition he's doing to represent the studio and drum up some more business. The group chatted for a bit about it, and then somehow Luke and I ended up with our own private text message exchange. Again, all business at first: he mentioned how I was already working that night and going to the competition afterwards would be cutting it close. He didn't want me to feel obligated or rushed. I said that wasn't possible and that I'd be there.

Hours passed and then he texted again, this time with zero pretense that it was work related.

> My laundry service place went out of business

He added a gif of a small child breaking down in agony.

> YOU PAY TO HAVE YOUR LAUNDRY DONE?!

The conversation went from there about how it was an old habit left over from college, but he was going to venture out into the real world and go to an actual laundromat. Teasing ensued, and he was a good sport about it. Our texting topics evolved from laundry, to college, to cooking, and then to dancing. I was mostly fine throughout the conversation, but once we started talking about our love for all forms of dancing, I was done for.

Male dancers have always been the rare crack in my otherwise impenetrable armor against love. It's the confidence and passion that do me in every damn time. Some random dude from the restaurant or from a bar? I'll have a one-night-stand where no one spends the night and we never see each other again. A bit of flirting beforehand, a hefty amount of foreplay, and then a few rounds in the sheets, and I'm good. I never have to see the guy again. I likely won't even remember his name, and depending on where and how he met me, he likely never knew my real name to begin with.

But dancers? I drool just thinking about Luke on the pole. His lean muscular body hoists itself up as if weightless. It's intimate, too. As if watching someone confront their inner demons, where sometimes they come out victorious, but just as often, they don't. His features are in line with whatever is happening with the music and his movements. I know all of this because some of the text thread contains videos of himself, videos I maybe watched a few too many times. Though really it would have been rude not to since he sent them and asked for suggestions on which songs and pole moves he should include in the contest.

This is his first contest, and he's going as a representative of the studio. A way to bring in both men and women as new clients. Now it all makes sense why he said Calista was pressuring him so much. It wasn't pressure from a boss only, but also as an older sister who feels entitled to demand more from family. I saw the same at the restaurant with Diesel's three kids, who all did their time as hostesses as soon as they hit 16. No preferential treatment there; he worked them the hardest.

I set the phone on the couch next to me, on the other side, so that it's no longer between us.

"I enjoy flirting with the sexy dancer," I admit, owning up to the few times I let the conversations slip into playful banter about mounting poles. "I won't apologize for that."

"No one's asking you to, and no one's shaming you." At the idea of that, her expression changes to shock and anger. "Holy crap. Are the people at work shaming you? Is that bitch Sonya being extra nice about your post pole hook-ups?

Did she offer you a pretty pink condom or something equally thoughtful?"

Fuck, she's good. I can always count on Paige to lighten a mood.

"No, no one suspects anything at work, and there's nothing to suspect because nothing is happening."

"So you think he's hot and you like him, but you're not sleeping with him. Why, Anna Laurier," Paige says, channeling her inner Scarlet O'Hara, "I do declare you actually like this guy. I never thought I'd see the day."

Crap. I do actually like this guy. How is it that I needed to hear Paige say it for me to realize it? I'm not just keeping him at arm's length because it'll interfere with my primary goal. I'm doing it to protect the both of us. Because Jessi, the woman he's working so hard to win over, she doesn't even exist.

"Yes, maybe a little," I concede. "But again, nothing is happening between us and nothing can happen between us. He's not interested in me; he's interested in Jessi." I grab a comforting handful of cheesy crackers and we both quietly contemplate for a minute. "You won't tell Calista, will you?"

It would be unimaginable for this to all abruptly end tomorrow, with me begging Diesel to give me my hours back and never returning to Art of Spinning. Sure, I could theoretically continue my pole journey at another studio, sans Calista's help, but who can afford that? Studios charge top dollar for these classes and I'd be back down to my single income of mostly tips from tourists.

"You said there was nothing to tell. Besides, she's ghosted me again," Paige says with more than a hint of sadness in her voice. "She's been busier than usual lately, I guess. Probably back to setting up that new location now that she's getting closer to straightening out her financial stuff."

We sip our wine until I can't ignore this nagging feeling. Without giving it too much thought, I put it out there. "You asked earlier if there was anything to report. There was this one-off moment on my first day there, where someone mentioned the cameras in the rooms and then it felt like everyone got weird about it."

Paige's head snaps towards me. "There are cameras? Like, in all the studio rooms, or just the lobby and out front?"

Well, fuck. Paige's reaction was more intense than I expected, and now I really don't know what to make of it. Is it me? Am I secretly some sort of exhibitionist who doesn't mind the cameras while everyone else's unhinged reaction is normal? Because Paige looks an awful lot like Luke right now.

"Yeah, they're all over the studio. Luke does the studio's tech stuff, too. He said they set them up a few months back as a sort of safety precaution for instructors and students. Why do you look like that? Is there something I should know? What am I missing?"

She scoffs and rolls her eyes, her way of laughing off her initial gut response. "No, that makes complete sense. Lots of limited clothing, seductive dancing, mood lighting... I get it."

"Right. But it got weird when I brought it up, and then people tensed up when I implied Calista was flighty for mentioning them to me when she first hired me."

Paige thinks it over for a minute. "Was her brother there when you mentioned it?"

I sigh. For the past two weeks I've convinced myself that I was on to something, getting closer by the day to whatever dirty little secret is wreaking havoc on Calista's tenuous financial situation. This one brief conversation with Paige has me right back at square one.

Reading my silence she says, "No sane person is going to talk smack about the boss in front of the boss's family."

I'm going to have to double my efforts. I hope my body enjoyed this one evening off from the pole, because it's my last until I get this thing sorted out. Calista hasn't put too much heat on me yet, but it's only a matter of time. And my bank account could use another little bump. Too much of that initial lump sum went to bills and expenses I'd been putting off for the past few years.

"Now," she continues with a wicked grin, "speaking of Luke…"

"There's nothing to speak of."

"I believe there is with that text message asking for your help after-hours at the studio."

Right. That. What am I going to say back to that?

CHAPTER 10
LUKE, FRIDAY, JULY 12TH

"What'd she say?" Travis asks, plopping down next to me on the bench at the laundromat.

When I don't immediately answer, Gabe chimes in from his spot on the other side of the bench. "See, I told you it was a bad idea. Too soon; too direct."

"It's not," Trav argues back. The two of them are talking as if I'm not sitting right between them. "It shows confidence, and women dig a confident guy who goes after what he wants."

The older gentleman sitting on the other side of Gabe, the one shamelessly eavesdropping on our conversation and making eye contact while he's doing it, gives a nod and a thumbs-up to Trav.

I ignore all of it and don't point out that they're both with me, their roommate, on a Friday night, doing laundry, and therefore are probably not the best to be doling out dating advice. Same with the older man. I don't see a wedding ring on that hand he just used to support Trav's bogus theory.

Instead, I'm staring at my message thread with Jessi, willing those three dots to appear so she can either make my night or put me out of my misery.

"She read it," I tell them, "but nothing back yet." Then I shove my phone in my pocket so I don't resort to stalking her response all night. I also don't need to spend another night reviewing all our texts, looking for clues about who this woman really is and if she'd ever take a chance on a guy like me.

Because right now, I'm getting a lot of mixed messages. During that first class, I kept catching her watching me. Granted, I was the instructor, and she was there to learn how to run the class. But the way her eyes locked in on me was not the stuff student gazes are made of. I should know. I teach plenty of these classes and very few of the women ever look at me like that. Not that I'm not incredibly good-looking and charming–just ask my older female relatives who still pinch my cheeks at holiday meals–but because the students are usually there for themselves, not to pick up guys. So yes, throughout class I felt like I was potentially getting signals from her, even though she seemed to have cooled down when we were having drinks with the others.

Just when I was about to brush it off as wishful thinking on my part, I helped her up from the couch and there was a moment. We almost kissed. I'm sure that had I leaned in, just enough to get me halfway there, she would have met me in the middle. The sexual tension was palpable.

Don't even get me started on what happened during the photo shoot. There was heat and energy and chemistry all in that brief session where she posed, and I mostly took pictures with only occasional skin-to-skin contact when I needed to help her into a specific position. She felt it, too. I know it. I saw and felt the goosebumps on her skin, the blush on her cheeks, and then for the tiniest hint of a second, there was a damn fire in her eyes. That one I'm sure about because I caught it with my camera. Have lost myself in those eyes late at night scrolling through the few photos I kept on my phone.

So why is she keeping me at bay? Not letting me ride the

subway with her after that first late-night class, not staying after class to chat with me since that first day, and now potentially turning down my request for her help in tightening up my dance routine. Maybe the age thing, but she doesn't seem like the type to be weirded out by that. It's more likely Calista gave her the same lines about not fraternizing at work.

If so, I'm screwed. Jessi takes professionalism to a whole new level. It's the beginning of a new job, so I get that she's showing her best self right now, but I haven't seen such devotion to the art of pole work since, well, me. Jessi's never running into the studio at the last minute, never even mildly unpleasant to any staff or clients, and she practically lives here with all the extra classes she joins and studio time she carves out. It's made my own newfound devotion to spending more time here that much more tolerable, but it's killing my resolve.

I flirt shamelessly–how could I not? Every day there's something else I notice about her or see or hear that makes me fall a little bit harder. Sitting at the desk and listening to the muffled sounds of her playlists during class, watching her teach as I pretend to casually check the cameras, and watching her determination as she tries more difficult moves in my pole strengthening classes.

Since we can't flirt too openly at the studio without garnering the attention of everyone else, especially Florence, we've subtly transitioned to text messages. Why not? It's harmless fun since we're both bound by Calista and other various factors to never act on it.

But even with the extra time at the studio and the texting, I want to know more. I want to know everything and I'm not above online stalking. Too bad she's a digital ghost.

Gabe's sister stopped by the other night and confirmed there's nothing. Jessi's name randomly came up in conversation (I brought it up because I'm intrigued and I can't stop thinking about her) and his sister Nora took it upon herself to use her feminine social-media-searching superpowers to help me out. No luck. There is literally nothing. Plenty of handles with the name Jess, Jessi, or Jessica Brown in NYC, but their pictures obviously didn't match, or the content overall was clearly not a good fit given what little I do know about the woman.

Based on our text messages these past weeks–all initiated by me, sadly–I know she prefers maple frosted doughnuts, her favorite artist to dance to is Doja Cat, and she's allergic to cats. Her father's been out of the picture since she was a child, and she never sees her mother, though I don't know if that's because of the distance or if there's some sort of rift with a long backstory to go with it.

Based on my experiences with her, I know she can start up a conversation with just about anyone. She isn't afraid to be in uncomfortable situations, like partnering up with Ellen and learning pole, given some of what's involved with pole dancing. And I know she can laugh at herself like when she made those inappropriate comments at the coffee shop and when she knee-planted before our first class.

In fact, I think that's what I like most about her, is that while she's possibly overly serious about her work, she doesn't take herself too seriously. I've known people who are deathly afraid of embarrassment; the mere prospect of it prevents them from taking on any risks in life. Take pole dancing, for example. I started when I was in high school. I'd seen Calista practicing, had been to the studio when she was getting ready to open for business, and I was hooked. While my friends eventually embraced my love for it, and sometimes even showed a bit of interest in trying out a move or two–when no one else was around–none of them had ever considered taking a class or doing anything in public. They were happy to get concussions each Friday night out on the football field, but out of fear of embarrassment, they couldn't put themselves out there to try out a sport that's predominantly filled with women and some-times strippers.

My pocket vibrates, and I know. Before I even take my phone out to confirm it, I know she's politely turning me down.

> I have a lot going on. Ask Sonya. She's always eager to help

I chuckle at that. I've seen Jessi's expressions whenever she's around Sonya, so I know damn well she is not a fan though she hides that for the most part. I doubt Sonya has any idea.

> Yeah, I'll do that

> But it won't be nearly as fun without you there

"Dude..." Gabe says, reading over my shoulder.

"What?"

"That's weak." Gabe reads the conversation for Trav to hear, and now the two guys who have never had a woman over to the apartment in the year and a half we've been living together are arguing over how best to proceed.

Trav, a thirty-year-old who's had no girlfriends *in his life*, says, "Send a message telling her you're taking her out to a fancy restaurant. You need to word it in a way that she can't say no. Even better, tell her you won't take no for an answer."

The older gentleman, evidently feeling bolder now since he has all his laundry done and is ready to leave anyway, says, "That's exactly what you do. Wear her down. Women always say no before they say yes." With a wink, the man is out of the laundromat and I have the urge to watch him walk down the street, making sure he doesn't encounter any women on his way home.

"It's not a business deal, and I'm not doing anything, ever, that's going to limit a woman's ability to say no," I say in response. Trav always claims he's too busy for girlfriends and that he'll have plenty of time for them once he's gotten a promotion or two, but I doubt it. As a roommate, Trav's great: he's never at the apartment because he puts in insane hours at work, and he's a neat freak. As a guy, he's toxic, and Gabe and I both call him out for that shit.

"Seriously, Trav, you are fucked up in the head when it comes to women. Do better," Gabe says before turning to me for his next bit of advice. "And *you* need to lay it out and accept her decision, or back the fuck off. It's been two weeks. You're going to do something beyond flirting, or you're not."

"I know, and I'm going to. We both have a class Sunday night. If nothing happens before then, I'll lay it all out after class."

"We'll see," he says with a hand up and his eyes focused across the room. Clearly our conversation is over and he is now more interested in his own love life as he checks out the two women who just arrived.

"Go on, then. Show us how it's done, Gabe," Trav says in a lowered tone so as not to scare off the ladies.

I take a deep breath as I contemplate the choices in my life that have me here, doing laundry with my single roommates, on a Friday night.

I could be at the studio, but the only thing happening tonight is karaoke, and I'm kind of in agreement with Jessi when it comes to Sonya. I love her to death and we have a history of sorts, but she is a bit much. It's not just the constant pep, but the way it bleeds into everything else. Like tonight's music theme for karaoke pole: "There's Always Tomorrow." As in every song is uplifting and optimistic and from the 20th century. Some clients love it and think the themes match the energy of the studio. At the same time, some of our clients are here to reclaim their voice and they're dying for aggressive, take-back-their-autonomy themed nights, like "Revenge Pole." I already have the Spotify playlist set up and more than a few students who are interested, just waiting on the green light from the boss. If only she was around or returning calls and text messages.

While Trav harasses Gabe, who's still too chicken shit to get up and approach the cute woman on the other side of the laundromat who's waved back to him, I glance down at my phone and notice those fabulous little dots dancing around on the screen.

> I signed up to teach the late-night intro class. Looks like I'll be the last one there. Do I need a key or something to lock up?

My mind replays back to a recent memory of me telling Trav how I'd never deceive a woman into a yes, but here I am tricking her into taking on a class where I would be the solo student. My stomach does that thing where it feels like I'm on an amusement park ride and my insides are rising while the rest of me plummets to the ground at life-threatening speeds.

Gabe said it best. I need to come out with it all and see where it lands me. Sure, he's spineless now, wiping his sweaty hands on his jeans and then pretending to inspect the dryer next to us rather than have a quick conversation with the opposite sex. But if it comes down to advice from Trav and the random old dude, or Gabe, I'm going to go with Gabe every time. I'm also putting down "expanding my circle of friends" on my checklist of things to do.

My thumbs hover over the keypad. I don't know how to explain this, especially in a text message, so I bite my lower lip—a habit I do anytime I'm about to do something physically or mentally painful—and then I let it loose.

> The class is for me

I shoot that one off quickly before I can take it back. I type again right afterwards, so she knows there's more coming. I only hope she'll keep reading beyond the first message.

> I overheard you saying you wanted to pick up other classes for a bit of extra cash and so I made one up. Knowing you'd take it. I figured you could help me get ready for Pole Masters

> Then I marked it in the system as full even though I was the only student

> It was supposed to be cute and funny but now I'm thinking it makes me look like a weirdo and I promise I'm not

I pause. The three dots bounce in sync with my left leg. The dots disappear, then they reappear, then they disappear again.

I'd ask Gabe for advice, but he found his balls and is now on the other side of the room, deep in conversation. I don't dare disturb him.

As a Hail Mary, I type one last message, a reminder that there's some sort of connection between us she hopefully can't deny.

> I was going to ask Sonya like you said. But she's too sunshine and rainbows

> I need someone who's not afraid to tell me I'm fucking something up

I wait again. There are way too many messages from me with no responses from her. Ball's in her court. I flip the phone over on my leg, expecting to sweat it out for the next few minutes when it vibrates again.

> You're fucking this up

I've heard the line before, about releasing a breath you didn't know you were holding. But has anyone unclenched an asshole they didn't know they were clenching? Because that odd sensation just happened to me, and I think I get the releasing the breath line. Kind of.

I smile back at the phone. Even if I wasn't interested in her, I'd still be desperate to have her over anyone else to help me prepare. This competition goes beyond Calista trying to drum up more business for the studio. Pole dancing is slowly becoming more popular with people seeing it not just as half-naked women with nipple tassels, and more as the sport that it actually is. A sport I want to prove myself in.

Our machines go off signaling the last loads in the dryers are done. Time to wrap this up and get the hell out of here. Doing laundry out in the wild is overrated. I'll be going back to dropping it off for washing and folding–totally worth the extra money and hassle of finding a new company.

> See? This is why I need you

> You tell me when. I'm at your mercy

More dots come and go and I'm dying to know what she's deleting and rewriting. When I'm texting Gabe or Trav, the dots never disappear. We fire off whatever random thought comes to our mind. Writing and rewriting responses is a good sign. I think.

"Let's go, jackasses," Trav calls to me and Gabe. He's already halfway done folding while I'm fucking around on the bench, and Gabe's wrapping up a conversation with the ladies, taking his phone back from the brunette who seems to have put her number in. He's practically giggling when he's back at the table and folding his underwear. Good thing our backs are to them now; the man has zero chill.

"D'you seriously get a date at the laundromat?" Trav asks in a hushed voice, leaning in so they don't overhear our conversation.

"Yeah," Gabe says with a shrug, as if he's always getting numbers from attractive women. He's full of shit because he still has a crazy grin on his face and this isn't the first time we've hung out together outside of the apartment, but it is the first time he's ever gotten a number. "We're doing dinner and drinks next week."

"No, shit," I say, with a congratulatory nudge to his arm. "Well played."

"I told you. Now hurry up and finish. I told them we had plans later tonight," Gabe says, his clothes only somewhat folded and organized as he shoves them back into the bag he brought. "If it comes up, we're going to a party."

Trav snorts. "You're so full of shit. What other lies did you tell her to get her number?"

"None, now move it. The longer we stay here, the more chances you'll fuck this up for me."

"Me?" Trav says, his progress halted as both his hands are now up and pointing to his chest.

"You, motherfucker," Gabe mutters as he shoves the last of Trav's clothes in the bag himself. "See you next week, Sasha," he calls as we head towards the doors.

She and her friend turn and give him a wave goodbye. "Yes, Tuesday. Can't wait to hear what you think of the book," the brunette calls out before we leave. She's holding up a well-worn copy of a paperback, little colorful tabs sticking out here and there.

"Yup, can't wait," Gabe says quickly before he practically shoves us out the door.

Like teenagers, Trav and I burst out laughing and start hooting and howling about Gabe's "date."

"It's a book club," Trav accuses between guffaws as we head home. "You don't even read." More laughter. "It's not a date. It's on a Tuesday."

Gabe shakes his head, unbothered by Trav's very accurate assessment of the situation. "Fuck off. That's how it's done. She's not just going to go out on a date with some guy hitting on her at the Wash Station. Book club's a safe place. Lots of people around and it takes the pressure off us. It's perfect. She's perfect."

"Right, perfect," I say with a straight face. "Except now you have to read the book. Do you even know how to read?"

I'm the only person in the apartment with a small stack of books on my nightstand. They're all loans from the library because space is limited and I don't have the luxury of having a bookcase. Trav reads mostly reports and non-fiction business-type books like *The Entrepreneur Mind,* but even that's only once or twice a year.

Gabe's more of a historical podcast type of guy. If the club is reading historical fiction, he might be okay. But generally, Gabe is always on the move. Unless there's an audiobook version he can listen to while working out or commuting to work, I don't see this happening for him.

"I read all the time," Gabe spits back, his words trailing off at the end as his conviction in his lie wanes. "I mean, I could read more if I had the time. Now, I'm going to make time. Come on," he says, leading us a longer way home even though we're trudging around with giant bags of clothing slung over our shoulders. "I need to stop at the newsstand."

While Trav and Gabe are inside, I pull my phone out to find a message from Jessi.

> Tomorrow night. I have a class until 9:30. I'll help you after

It's painfully formal and lacking anything that could be considered flirtatious, but I'll take what I can get. She's overlooked my previous nefarious plotting and offered to help, regardless. Besides, she's probably out-and-about enjoying her Friday night off. I like that she won't blow off whatever she's up to to spar back and forth with me.

> Perfect. See you then

Gabe comes back out of the store and before he even realizes what's happening, Trav snatches the book from his hands and is reading the back cover as we start the last block home.

"Cassandra Thorello, a peasant living in the alleyways of the East End, has just passed through a portal into the world of Vontel. After narrowly avoiding being eaten by feral dragons, she's captured by a clan of virile fairies who lock her up in the highest tower of their castle to be used as they wish. That is, until Magnus, the fairy leader, starts to fall for the no-nonsense heroine and decides he's done sharing her with anyone. Now, the two are up against the entire kingdom as they try to escape Vontel forever."

We've all stopped walking now, each of us is staring at the book still in Trav's hand. Our brows furrow as we try to comprehend what the giant tome of a book is about.

"It's…" I say, unsure of exactly how to word it. "It's fairy porn?"

Gabe has the book again and is on the move. "Sasha said there's a little bit of that, but that's only a few chapters," he calls over his shoulder since Trav and I are struggling to keep up while also laughing uncontrollably.

"And you think you're going to read that entire book before the meeting?" I asked, genuinely interested in how that could happen, given how much the guy works and works out.

"You, too?" Gabe turns to ask, his eyes locked on me. "We've been listening to your shit about Jessi for almost a month. Supportively listening. And you can't be encouraging the couple of blocks it takes to walk home? Absolute bullshit," he mumbles, shaking his head as he leads the way back to our place.

Trav and I continue laughing and fumbling our steps back to the apartment, but I know he's right. I pull my phone out again. I'm not up for another trip out, but I splurge and order Gabe a DoorDash order as part of the apology Trav and I will give him later once he's calmed down. On top of getting him his favorite pizza, I put in another order for Rite-Aid and select a set of mini Post-It tabs for him to mark up his new book, and I throw in a last-minute bottle of lotion, for the fairy porn part.

CHAPTER 11
ANNA, SATURDAY, JULY 13

Since I have the schedule memorized, I know Luke teaches classes from noon to six. So I'm surprised when I look up from helping a student in my 8:30 class and notice him already sitting against the back wall, watching me. I assumed he would escape the studio for a few hours before returning at the end of my class for our own private session.

He's wearing black sweat shorts, a gray tee that clings to his ripped arms and stomach, and those damn glasses. Pole has been quite the journey in self-discovery, but I think the most surprising thing I've discovered about myself is that I have a glasses kink. Who knew? His hair falls slightly over his forehead and when his eyes meet mine, I get an easy smile in response.

This man is going to be the death of me. *I* wasn't the one who accepted this one-on-one session with him late at night. That was the wine agreeing to such nonsense. For over a month, I'd cut back on booze almost completely, so two glasses with Paige last night left me more than buzzed.

I had a slight headache earlier while I was working the lunch shift at Papa Pizzano's, but I barely noticed it. All I could think about earlier today was how we would be alone in the studio, and how my sole responsibility while we were alone would be to watch him closely while he performed. I'll need to be acutely aware of where every part of his body is, how he's moving to the music, and how it's making me, the audience member, feel.

Basically, I'll be doing exactly what he's doing now. Because he's watching me like a hawk, as if I'm his prey. I feel his eyes on me while I'm working with Heather, a newbie to the pole dancing experience. It doesn't make me nervous the way I thought it might if he ever came into one of my classes. My confidence has only grown in the past few weeks. What I feel instead is the heat of his gaze and a feeling of impatience. After what felt like an entire day but was only 60 minutes, we're ready to do our end of session stretching and decompressing. It's a late class with an almost 10 o'clock end time. After stretching, the students are quick to leave and get back to whatever they have going on at home or back to their adventures out in the world. The past me would have envied them, would have created intricate histories and futures for these people that I could only dream about. And now, one month later, I'm pretty sure they'd envy me if they had any idea what was about to happen in the studio they so quickly vacated.

"You're good," Luke says once the last student is out the door, and it's only him and me in the now cavernous-feeling room. He's still seated against the wall, so I plop down next to him, my drink in hand.

"Thanks. I had an excellent teacher my first day."

"No." He shakes his head and brushes his hair off his forehead, even though it immediately falls right back down again. "I mean it. You're a natural instructor."

I take a swig of water and try to figure out how to respond. In the end, I settle on a shrug and some comments about how I enjoy doing it. On the inside, I'm dying. Why, oh why, do I lose my wit whenever Luke is in close proximity? I'm a fucking delight to be around with clever puns, comebacks, and more. But not when I'm one-on-one with him. My tongue feels like it's grown three times its size and my brain reverts to my toddler days with a finite understanding of how communication even works.

Mercifully, he gets down to it.

"Can I link up to the system?" he asks, pulling out his phone and opening Spotify. "I already warmed up in studio C so I wouldn't take up too much of your time."

"It's all yours. I'll lock up while you're setting up." I leave the room to make sure we're the only ones left in the building, I verify that no personal belongings were left behind, and then I lock the front door and turn out all the lights. We don't want any distractions from the outside world for the next few hours, or however long we're in the back room together. While I've already acknowledged this whole thing is a terrible idea, I've also somewhat conceded that I'm utterly defenseless when it comes to turning down Luke's advances.

I'm mentally prepared, and yet wholly unprepared, once I get back to the room and find Luke at a pole in nothing but those tiny tight shorts. Nothing about this situation is unexpected, and yet my breath catches when I catch sight of that inked up, toned chest.

He's pleased to see me flustered. I can tell by the cocky-ass half smile he gives me. I can't blame him, though. Who doesn't enjoy having that effect on someone?

"Ready?" I ask, sliding my ass down to the floor once more as I rest my back against the wall.

"Are *you* ready?" he counters. Then he's walking towards me and I'm positive that this is it. We're going to skip anything related to his performance and instead we'll have passionate sex right here in the studio with the perfect lighting and the giant wall of mirrors. It's a scenario that's played out in my head, on a loop some nights when I can't sleep, even though my body and mind are both thoroughly spent. The lies I've told myself about how I would never allow this terrible mistake to happen? They're barely whispers, and the more I strain to hear them again, the softer they get.

"Can you hit play for me when I say when?" he asks as he hands me his phone.

"Mm-hmm," is all I can manage in response. I add, "I love this song," at the last second, so that I don't sound like an absolute moron. There's nothing fake about the comment, though. Walking down the street, cleaning up around the apartment, and dancing in my tiny living room, I have been listening to it practically on repeat, my mind always filling with visions of him and me doing all sorts of naughty things together.

"You're sure? Because I have a few backups, too. The bar's pretty rowdy and the winner's chosen by applause. The song is just as important as the dance."

Poor guy is asking a serious question about the music, and all I can think about is him laying in bed listening to some Fuck Me Slowly Spotify playlist trying to pick out the best song, and what would have happened if I had been laying in that bed with him. Would we have kept some sort of pace with the music, let it guide us in our exploration of each other, or would it have merely been the catalyst to spark the initial caresses and kisses that would inevitably turn into something all its own once the lust took over our brains.

"No," I tell him. "'Slow Hands' is the perfect song, and I know the bar you're talking about. I haven't been there for any of their competitions, but I know the general crowd. Those twenty-something year olds watching you, on the pole, imagining you're performing just for them, and thinking how there's no chance you're leaving without them..."

I trail off at the end of that statement because it hit way too close to home and he can tell. It's me; I'm the one imagining he's performing that song just for me and that maybe there's no chance he'll leave without me tonight.

He gives a slow grin that I can't quite read and says something about how his roommate made a similar comment. Roommate? What roommate? Male? Female? I'm jealous either way if Luke is like Calista and has a few poles in his apartment that he's been using to show off all his moves to this roommate. Fortunately, there isn't time to spiral on that right now. He's at the pole and waiting for the green light from me.

I know I'm in trouble, but I press the start button anyway. I told Paige there could never be anything between Luke and me, but even as I was saying it, I knew that was a lie. This moment between us is inevitable, and with the touch of my thumb on the phone, we've entered the next level of the will-we-won't-we game we've been playing.

CHAPTER 12
LUKE, SATURDAY, JULY 13

As difficult as it is, I completely put Jessi out of my mind when I'm on the pole. It's the only way I know how to do it, and from what I've seen of her, Jessi's the same way. One minute I'm zeroed in on every aspect of her: her soft brown hair, which has a faint smell of honey from her shampoo or whatever hair product she uses, is now in a ponytail, and there's a tiny thread coming off the bottom of the faded Under Armour sweat shorts she's thrown over her bottoms. She's worrying the lower left corner of her lip like she has something on her mind but won't say it.

The next minute, the music is going and I'm the only one in the room. I worried at first that maybe this wasn't such a good idea, fraternizing with coworkers, but I really do need legit critiquing on my dance, and Jessi is hands-down the best one to give it to me. As much as I want to appease Calista–even though she is decidedly unappeasable lately–I also want to do this for myself. I've been to the Velvet Lounge for their competitions and it's cut-throat. This isn't one of those instances where anyone can sign up the day before or night of and give it their best shot. There are three stages of auditions to get through beforehand. I'll be going up against other guys who are potentially more experienced than I am.

It's been a pain in my ass and this was my fourth time auditioning before I finally got into the competition, but I need this validation. I need a crowd of people blown away by my talent with no mention or focus on my gender. Not that I'm not playing that up to my advantage. Like I told Jessi, picking "Slow Hands" was intentional, as are my moves. I incorporated a string of difficult inversions as a bit of showboating, but I also made sure I had time on the ground for some more sensual movements to match the song and the atmosphere.

This competition, based on the events I've attended in the past, is kind of like pole Olympics with a touch of *Magic Mike*, if such a thing existed. Not that I or anyone else that will compete anywhere near Olympic or Channing Tatum status, but the difficulty level is significantly higher than what the average person expects to see when they hear "pole dancing."

Before I know it, the song is winding down and with a gentle landing on the balls of my feet, I'm back on the floor with my gaze stuck on a random spot a few feet in front of me. Jessi's opinion matters; I need that extra chunk of time to reorient myself and prepare for her reaction.

When I do look, my one hand still resting on the pole since I'm glued to this spot while I await my fate, she's wide-eyed with her lips in a sort of pinched or pursed position. Either it was amazing, and she's about to let loose with a string of compliments, or she's sorting through some major criticism and wondering how she's going to let me down gently. I'd sent her some videos before, but they were merely quick clips. I was so critical of myself I'd only send stuff to her if I thought it was perfect, and very few videos met that standard.

"Well?" I finally say, taking my hand off the pole and walking towards her.

At that, she stands up and walks to meet me halfway, her hands busy adjusting her ponytail. "Your inversions are good, and I don't even know the names of half the moves you did up there to adequately comment on them, but they were all great, too."

"But?" I ask, because I can tell there's a but. Letting go of her hair, she's now playing with her fingers the same way she did at the coffee shop that first day.

"Your entrance is flat. If this was a true pole competition based on nothing but your skills, you'd kill it. But it's not. You need to woo around a hundred drunk, ready-for-a-show women and men." When I don't immediately respond, she adds, "Again, I can't do half of what you did. It's amazing; truly. But you need to play to your audience, too, and you're not. Not yet."

At this, I have to agree. There's a moment in the song where the momentum builds and I transition from position to position as I quickly spin around the pole, but that's at the two-minute mark, towards the end, with my ground work coming afterwards. Everything before then would be a slow-tension building before the grand finale of sorts. Jessi's idea of blowing them away at the beginning? That makes more sense. If I have a three-minute song, I need to make the most of all of it. I need them screaming from the first beat, not heading to the bar to get a fresh drink.

"Yeah, I see what you're saying." I think it over for a second. "I could come in with a double reverse grab into a phoenix." I'm already on my way back to the pole before I even finish saying it. After a half rotation, I'm in the air with only one arm holding me up. As I spin, I add the other hand just above the ground so I'm turning with both hands on the pole, my grip going beyond my shoulders, and my body off to the side before raising my hips and legs above me.

My spin finally stops, leaving me facing Jessi, upside

down and holding the pose like it's nothing. My shameless attempt at impressing her.

"Not like that," she says, as if I've just done a somersault in a gymnastics class.

I hide my disappointment in my dismount.

"That looked amazing," she clarifies, signaling that I did not hide my disappointment in my dismount, "and I do think you should use that to start on the pole, but I'm talking about your floor work."

"I already have floor work. Besides, it's mainly a pole competition…" I trail off at the end, unsure of where her confusion is coming from and how to address it.

"And like I said, you're going to crush the pole part of it. What you're going to fail miserably at is making the ladies scream louder than front-row Swifties."

"Should I have picked a Taylor Swift song?!"

She gives a soft chuckle that makes me feel like Superman and says, "Under different circumstances, maybe." Jessi eyes up my body: up and down, then up and down again. "What else are you going to be wearing?"

I put my arms out and spin as if I'm showing off a tux when really all I'm wearing is a black pair of biker shorts that hide nothing.

"Do you still have the professor outfit? And your glasses?"

"Nope," I say, shaking my head, knowing where this is going. I have my jacket and button down in the cubby in the chill room. It's my go-to outfit most days just for the simplicity of it, but also because I found people take me more seriously when I have on the jacket and the glasses. I already look younger than I am, so wearing something a tad aging has been helpful. But I've *never* considered using it in the way she's insinuating.

"Come on," she says, unconvinced. "Have you really never mixed pole dancing and stripping?"

And now I'm picturing *her* mixing pole dancing and stripping, so I put my eyes anywhere else in the room. Jessi's outfit today is a strappy red top and strappy black bottoms with one strap that goes around her upper thigh, almost like a garter. No dick twitches today, thank you. I'm on full display and there'd be no way to hide that.

"In front of an audience of strangers? Never." Now there's a flash in her eyes, and I'm wondering if she's picturing me stripping. Not that she even has to since it sounds like that's where this conversation is heading and I already know I can't say no to this woman.

"It won't be all strangers. You invited all the instructors and half the clients at the studio. Dance for them."

"When you put it that way. Sure, I'll strip for all my coworkers and clients. That won't be awkward the next day."

Her eyes drop to my shorts, then back up to my eyes where she peers into my soul. "How are you such a prude in that tiny outfit?"

Calista and I have had this conversation numerous times. For over a year she and I have been focused on how to bring new clients into the studio, so we've gone back and forth about where we want to focus our efforts: the average person who's interested in learning pole as a fun and physically challenging hobby, or the average sex-worker who is looking to advance their skills in order to advance their career.

Calista won't admit it, but I think Mom is still swaying her opinion on this one. In her desperate attempt to win over Mother's approval, Calista is determined to minimize our association with anything related to sex work, and instead tries to emphasize the other aspects of pole dancing: how it's challenging physically, how it allows for creative expression, and how it helps build lean muscle. All the things Calista had to repeat over and over again to Mom and Dad when she was first planning to open her business and was going to ask them to co-sign on her business loan. Before the inheritance.

In the end, she didn't need their approval via a loan signature, but I think Calista is still holding out faith that they'll one day magically realize that they are, in fact, interested in their kids and their hobbies. So she insists we keep our dance studio image on the off chance they come around.

Before I can explain to Jessi how Calista and I already had the stripping-during-the-competition conversation and decided to focus on pole skills over floor work, Jessi launches into it.

"You're wearing next to nothing." She points at my dick, which is indeed covered only by a thin layer of fabric, the outline of my favorite body part there for everyone to see. "I promise you, doing a few sexy moves to take off extra clothing until you're down to your current outfit isn't as scandalous as you think it is."

The fight in me starts to dissipate. I would love nothing more than to seduce this fabulous, sexy woman, so I'll play along. I'm not convinced this is a good idea for Pole Masters, but I am convinced this is the perfect segue into something more between Jessi and me. She wants a show? I'll give her a show.

"Queue up my song again, please. I'll go put on my *outfit*," I say, accentuating the word outfit with my tone and finger quotes for good measure.

When I come back into the room, the song is already playing and Jessi, dressed in prop clothing from the bin in the room, is facing the mirrors. She has her legs slightly spread past her hips and bent at the knees as she rolls her hips in a way that has my cock beginning for me to take action. Even though we are now fully clothed, it's all that much more sensual and intimate: the dim lighting, the music blaring, the anticipation of dancing and disrobing together. Our eyes will have to be trained on each other, watching every move to critique or imitate.

"Dance with me," she says, those full lips turning up into

a seductive smile and I can't tell if she's caught up in the moment or if this is some sort of Mrs. Robinson instance where she's successfully trying to seduce me. To be fair, she wouldn't even have to try. She had me at party in my pants.

She's perpendicular to the mirrors so she can see from the side how she looks. I step up behind her, leaving a foot or two between us. The song has the same beat more or less throughout, so we don't need to keep pausing and replaying. We can mess around with different moves throughout while it plays on a loop.

"Good," she says, watching me do hip rolls. "Shoulders up… Yup, just like that."

Damn, she's right. It's a minor adjustment, but where I looked somewhat hunched before, now the focus is all on my hips and the light pelvic thrusts. I may have her beat with pole moves, but I can tell she's about to school me with this part.

"Okay, now we're going to swing our hips."

Fuck me. I'm trying so hard not to put all my attention on how badly I want to reach out and pull her hips back so that perfect ass is pressed up against me as we sway together. I'm supposed to be watching so I can imitate what she's doing, but my body has two different brains in my two different heads, and they both have only indecent thoughts running through them.

"Luke?" She stops moving, and it's enough to snap me out of it.

"Huh?" I'm back in grade school where the teacher would call on me, but I hadn't been paying attention for the last thirty minutes, so all I can muster in response is a monosyllabic sound that's borderline a grunt.

Over her shoulder, she gives me a once over, assessing the situation and where she should go from here.

I give a nervous, sheepish laugh and lie when I say, "I was getting there."

"Okay, let's try it this way." She turns to face me and takes the few steps needed so she's right in front of me. "Do you mind?" she asks as she holds out her hands, ready to place them on my hips. It comes with the territory, I know. We're careful here about boundaries and consent; there is zero touching allowed between instructors and clients. She's completely serious when she asks me if I mind, but I have to wonder, is she really not sure? Does she have any idea how long I've been waiting to have some sort of physical contact with her aside from that one time my knuckles grazed the back of her hand and when I moved her arm up for a picture?

"Not at all. I guess I can use all the help I can get," I say, acting as though I too wish it didn't have to come to this, and yet here we are. Just two people sensually dancing in a dimly lit room, late at night, reluctantly touching each other.

"Luke!"

"Huh?"

Her hands aren't quite at her sides, but they're also not touching me yet. She's looking at me expectantly. I start to sway my hips in time to the music again, assuming that's what she's waiting for.

"Yes, okay. Good," she says, amusement filling her voice and easing my anxiety at how twice, in the past five minutes, I've responded to this interesting, wonderful woman with "huh."

"Now," she says, eyeing up my swaying hips, "you want to take what you're already doing, and slowly swing your butt back and around, shifting the weight back and forth from one leg to the next, but nice and slow. No need to rush anything."

Ignoring her last words, blood rushes to my cock as soon as those perfect hands rest on my hips to guide them. There is zero chance of me being able to think unsexy thoughts right now, not with her touching me while I gyrate my hips, not with Niall singing about slow hands, and certainly not with the way her hooded eyes are focused on my… glasses? Interesting. Glad I put them back on as part of the outfit.

"How quickly can you loosen the tie and get it over your head?" she asks. Now I really like where this is going.

"A few seconds." We're still dancing, her hands still on my hips but not guiding them quite as much since I'm learning the rhythm and almost have it on my own. My hands, which had been somewhat useless before while I focused on my lower body, loosen my tie, pull it over my head, and hold it out for her as a meek offering of sorts.

She shakes her head. "Swing it around on your finger and then fling it out to the audience." We're at what would be considered the front of the room, so I look to the back where our theoretical audience would be and chuck my tie. It lands unceremoniously; a bit anticlimactic versus what the intended outcome at the bar will be.

"At the competition, I'm not getting that tie back, am I?"

"You are going to make some woman or man's night when they go home from the bar with a complimentary tie from the hot dancer."

I cock an eyebrow at her but don't verbally question her assessment as we continue to rock back and forth on our legs, our hips swaying to the music as if it's second nature now.

"You're good," I say. "Did they teach you this in Juilliard?"

"Strip Tease 101. I remember the class fondly."

Her hands leave my hips and I'm pleasantly surprised to find them now on my chest, fiddling with my buttons.

"These won't do. I'll show you with my shirt."

I feel the absence of her hands and her body as she pulls away from me. Now that there's distance between us again, I stop my own rhythmic motion to focus on her.

"You walk out," she says, "and immediately start with the shaking of the hips leading into the swaying back and forth, just like we were doing."

She's fully covered with a button down and tear-away pants, but even with the baggy clothing that doesn't match or really fit her at all, she's all together stunning. Anyone can tell she has a dancer's body underneath, and she knows how to use it.

"Then you loosen your tie and seductively fling it out to the crowd." She pantomimes that part since she doesn't have a tie. There's a tiny little lick lip before she says, "You'll have fake glasses, fling those down on the floor. Don't throw them out into the crowd. You don't want to knock someone in the head with them."

I nod my agreement. Here at the Art of Spinning, we take safety seriously.

"Now, once the tie and glasses are off, you reach up for the top of your shirt, right at the collar, like this."

I've already seen her without her shirt on, wearing nothing but the skimpiest of pole tops and bottoms, and yet the anticipation is overwhelming. Am I drooling? I wish I could check without being obvious and coming off like the absolute creep that I am. She's trying to help me, but how am I supposed to keep my mind out of the gutter when she's literally stripping in front of me?

"Go ahead," she says. "You won't actually take it off this round; pretend to as you're copying what I'm doing."

Once my hands are in place and I'm mentally prepared for her to rip her shirt off, she still doesn't.

"As you're ripping your shirt open, you're going to take a step forward, as if your naked torso is getting closer to them at the same rate you're losing articles of clothing."

We do it together a few times, slowly. Our hands start at our collars, we step forward, and as we're taking that one step, we pretend to pull down and out on the fabric, miming what it would look like to actually rip our shirts off. It is decidedly unsexy when broken down like this, just like most of the pole moves are when we're first learning them.

Jessi stops, her hands on her hips as she looks me over. I stop, too. She reaches up for my jacket collar and she's rubbing it between her thumb and fingers as if sizing up the material.

"Not sure about the professor's coat?" I ask, letting my pitch lower to something a little more intimate. "Seemed like you were pretty into it before."

"I've never been more sure of anything in my life. I'm just trying to figure out how to get it off of you." She nibbles at her lower lip and says, "What if when you first started, you eased it off your shoulders, and then let it fall the rest of the way as you increase your pace and booty shaking?"

"I can do that." Once I find the beat again, I hook my thumbs under my coat and ease it off my shoulders, just like she described. With my arms bent, the fabric catches at my elbows, and it takes some shimmying and relaxing of my arms before it falls to my feet.

"Perfect," she says, eying me up while I continue to dance. "Now, pretend to rip your shirt off and take the step, just like we practiced. Like this."

She falls in with the beat and seconds later she's lunging at me, tearing open her shirt and adding some sort of pelvic roll to top it all off. I don't mirror her. I don't do anything beyond taking in the moment. We're both standing still, and with her step towards me we're now face to face, our lips poised and ready for action. I can feel it; our eyes are locked and there's a pull between us, closing the short distance.

I can't say who initiates the next move. It's quite possible we both reached out at the same time. Her one hand lands on my chest, her thumb and fingers gently digging in and gripping the muscle in what can only be described as pure desperation, while the other goes for my jaw before quickly sliding to the back of my neck.

She hasn't taken her shirt off yet; it's still hanging open on her frame, an invitation for my hands to seek out her waist before exploring up her ribcage. When I slide my thumbs over her breasts and feel her tight nipples beneath her top, I hear her moan, feel the shot of air from her breath since our mouths are millimeters away from finally making contact.

"Where do I sign up for this class?" I hear someone call out over the music.

CHAPTER 13
ANNA, SATURDAY, JULY 13TH

'm not wearing anything unreasonable given that we're in a pole dancing studio, but I instinctively pull the shirt back in front of my chest and give a quick nonverbal thanks to the genius woman who invented the magnetic buttons that immediately catch, concealing me once again.

"Oh, hey, Sonya," I say, channeling my own version of Sonya where I'm trying to sound upbeat, my voice an octave or two higher than necessary as I fight for my life to be bubbly enough to match her energy. It's a 180 going from the absolute naughtiness that almost happened with Luke to being in a room with my unassuming coworker and a pack of her clients.

Luke and I weren't doing anything wrong, but the half-dozen people crowded in the doorway are all painfully aware of what they would have walked into had they shown up a few minutes later. One older woman gives me an appreciative nod, while the younger woman next to her can't pull her eyes away from Luke. I don't blame her. I'm often unable to pull my eyes away from that fine specimen of a man.

"Oh, hey, Jessi. Hey, Luke," Sonya parrots using the same upbeat tone.

Why, oh why, did it have to be Sonya? She's the only one at the studio that I haven't built up a strong relationship with. Anyone else I could explain how nothing happened or has happened with Luke and how I'd really appreciate them never, ever telling anyone else or bringing it up again. Ever. This can't get back to Calista.

This intrusion was the wake-up call I needed. I'm not merely risking pissing off my boss with a relationship with Luke. I'm jeopardizing the only thing that's brought pure joy to my life in over a decade. And for what? A guy I barely know? I can already hear the phone call coming my way, asking me why I'm fucking with her younger brother's heart when he doesn't even know my real name. Or much else about me.

He thinks I'm Jessi, a Juilliard graduate from a tiny town outside of Philly who's currently a thriving pole instructor. I'm growing into the latter as I did turn into one hell of an instructor, but the rest is all lies, and I know he's heard the other little white fibs I've been sprinkling around the studio the past few weeks.

No, Calista wouldn't like that at all and I can't blame her. Time for some damage control; time to regain my senses.

"We were just–" I say, but Luke cuts me off.

"Sonya, I didn't think you came in on Saturday nights," Luke says, shrugging his professor's jacket back on. It's only now that I realize how bizarre all of this is. What *is* Sonya doing here so late on a Saturday with a class of students? I don't know the time, but it has to be close to 11, if not later. There weren't any classes that late on the calendar; I would know. And how did she get in? I locked everything up. I'm sure of it.

"Ladies, go ahead and get changed. I'll be ready in a few minutes, and we'll get started," Sonya says, closing the door behind her so it's just the three of us left in the studio. As if

I'm one of the poles, Sonya goes straight for Luke and is speaking only to him.

"I'm in a bind," she says in a voice I don't recognize. It's full of desperation and despair and abject fear. "I'm so sorry. I said just one night a week, but then Theo had to go back to the hospital again. We're trying to make it on one income and we can't." Her voice cracks and I see the real Sonya underneath the bubbly facade. "You're not going to tell Calista, are you?"

Luke takes in those eyes brimming with tears and gives her a sad smile in return, his head shaking no before he can even vocalize it.

"Why didn't you tell me?" There's no anger. He's genuinely curious.

I have no business being here for this conversation, and I have no idea how to get out of it. Not that I want to. This is what I'm here for. To figure out whatever shady dealings are happening at the studio so I can report back to Calista. I pretend to fix my already immaculate magnetic buttons and try to blend in with the surrounding poles. Nothing to see here; please carry on with your deeply personal conversation about how you're having secret, late-night classes at the studio without Calista's knowledge.

"It's just a six-week class. I didn't want to bother you with it. I already had a key to the building, and you said the cameras weren't recording during off hours..."

"Jessi," Luke says, finally acknowledging my existence again.

I pull my eyes up from my buttons and give my best *who me?* look as if I had no idea other people were in the room.

"Can you give us a minute?"

"Yes, of course. Absolutely. Let me grab my phone and water, and I'll get out of your hair." I cringe inwardly at my use of the cliché, but I take my time walking over to collect my things before heading out. I was hoping they would start talking again, but they didn't. At least not in the way I was hoping.

"Jessi," Sonya calls out to me right before I reach the door. I turn around and give her what I hope is a look full of sympathy and concern. "I know," she says, her once pleading eyes now steely and boring into mine. "If you want me to keep your secret; I suggest you keep mine."

I put my hands up and take the final step backwards toward the door. "I'm not sure what you're talking about," I say, sweet as pie, "but I'm not telling anyone anything. I saw nothing tonight. Just like you." Before she can respond, I'm out the door.

I plop down behind the front desk to wait for Luke. As my mind races with what Sonya thinks she knows—my actual secrets or just the obvious that Luke and I have something going on—I power up the computer and look once more at the class schedule, specifically Sonya's classes.

Maybe she has friends who went to Juilliard and somehow knows I didn't go there. Except that wouldn't make sense given how big of a school it is, how she doesn't know the years I supposedly attended, and how my name is way too generic. Surely there was a Jessica Brown, maybe even a dozen, at Juilliard in the last decade or two. And my looks are average enough to match lots of other people since I'm of medium height with brown hair. The odds are in my favor with this one, so I dismiss that as a possibility.

The screen lights up and with a few clicks I'm at the calendar for June, July, and August. I'd somehow missed it before, but now I'm noticing Sonya leads the most classes and has a spread of both really early classes and the late evening classes. I look for anything beyond the 8:30 to 9:30 time slot and see nothing. The place should be deserted.

I wonder if this is the sort of thing Calista is looking for. Someone stealing her customers or using company space and equipment to teach off-the-books classes. It doesn't feel as good as I thought it would to crack the case. As much as I can only handle Sonya in the smallest of doses, and even though she offered me a veiled threat of sorts just minutes ago, it sounds like desperation and not greed is what led her here. I promised Sonya I wouldn't rat her out to Calista. They had been empty words at the moment, but the more I think about it, the more conflicted I am.

I close out the studio calendar. Before I completely power off the computer, I notice one of the file titles is not like the others. The folder names read Marketing, HR, Financials, Events, and Miscellaneous. What type of information would require a miscellaneous folder?

A few clicks later and I'm looking at what appears to be a poorly written business plan for a burlesque type dance studio. There's an entire document about the building loca-tion–it's this location–but there are multiple layouts that show the current rooms as they are, then the following three maps are the same address but with massive differences: walls taken down, walls put up, and gigantic bathroom areas that mirror the fantasies of most women.

I close out the "Layout" document and open another labeled "Staff."

It lists out all the staff members, including Florence. It has their current name and position, then there's a colon and on the other side of the colon, for at least half of the staff, there's a different name and a different position.

Lyric, Bachelorette Parties: Lyric, Bachelorette Parties

Mel, Inversion Instructor: Belvoir, Neo-Burlesque

Jessi, Intro Instructor: Anna, Classic Burlesque

Luke, Pole Strength and IT: Luke, Boylesque

Florence, Customer Service: Florence, Owner

Lux, Pole in Heels: Lux, Neo-Burlesque

There are no financials attached, no official business proposals, or anything else that signifies there's an actual plan in place to make these changes happen. But it's disturbing on numerous levels and I know I'm going to lose hours upon hours of sleep thinking about the implications of this document.

Florence isn't the only one on this computer, but she is the only one who uses it when there's down time. Under normal circumstances, there isn't any down time for instructors. If for some random reason they're here and not instructing, they often crash another person's class or use an open studio to practice or let loose. No one but Florence would be at the computer for longer than five minutes. And even then, if someone else was using it, Florence would likely be right by their side the entire time.

This must be her document.

But why are some instructors given alternative names, and why is my alternative name my actual name?!

And why is Florence the owner? She's never once seemed like the type of person who desperately wanted more responsibility. On the contrary, she seemed like the type of person who wanted as little responsibility as possible and was more or less here for the social aspect of it all. The type of person who didn't mind doing work, but also didn't mind getting paid to do her nails and create Etsy-type crafts at her desk.

Fuck. I was worried that I wouldn't be able to uncover anything wicked in this morally wholesome setting. A place purely devoted to informed consent when it comes to *any* touching, loving all bodies regardless of size, color, and gender, and a place where I've felt nothing but a familial connection with almost all of my coworkers. And then in one night I find out Sonya is secretly stealing customers, and Florence is at the desk plotting her takeover of, well, everything. I wonder if Luke knows the extent of it.

CHAPTER 14
LUKE, SATURDAY, JULY 13TH

insist on calling a cab this time and taking it with her back to her apartment. There's too much left unsaid, and it's late.

Jessi lives in Sunnyside, which gives us about 15 minutes in the backseat. Maybe more time if she invites me up, but the moment doesn't feel right anymore. She looks like she has a million things on her mind, while in the studio it felt like I was the only thing occupying her thoughts.

"So..." she says as the driver pulls away from the curb. "You and Sonya were a thing?"

I huff out a laugh. After everything that happened tonight, that was the last thing I expected her to say.

"No. There was never anything between Sonya and me, just secrets." There isn't any humor left in my voice. "I don't like to talk about it at work, ever, but Calista is my older sister." When I don't get the reaction I expected from her, I follow that up with, "But I'm guessing someone already told you..."

She nods. "Someone mentioned it, though I wish that someone would have been you."

I do, too. Looking back now, it feels stupid that I didn't.

That I ever told Calista to keep our familial relationship between us as much as possible.

"Yeah. Sorry about that. It's not just you; I hate being pigeonholed as the younger brother."

Jessi covers my hand with her own and gives it a supportive squeeze. "But that's not the secret you're talking about, is it?"

"No, it's not." I'm losing time. If she's not going to dwell on the brother-sister omission, then neither will I. "I've been working at my sister's studio for the past three years. The first few months were rocky and I'm still paying the price for some of my mistakes. One mistake in particular."

Jessi is waiting patiently for me to spill my secrets, and damn do I want to. She has this way about her where I never feel judged or inadequate. I don't worry about saying things to her and her not understanding. Granted, we haven't known each other long and I've mostly been on my best behavior around her as I've tried to win her affection. But I think, too, it's the way she's not too critical of herself that puts me at ease, believing she'll grant me the same leniency she grants herself.

Even now. She's in clothing that's seen better days, her hair has been through a day of work, and her makeup is less than perfect. As to be expected of someone who's worked their ass off all day and doesn't give a fuck what people think of appearances. Still, it's hard to find someone that comfortable in their skin and themselves. Or maybe I haven't been surrounding myself with the right kind of people. Either way, I've been wanting to unload this burden for years, so I decide not to hold back when Jessi offers the chance for me to engage in a taxi-cab back-seat confessional.

"Right. Um, I guess I'll start with how I started working at Art of Spinning."

I see the cab driver roll his eyes before calling back, "Let me know if you need me to take the long way. I have a few routes I use for these situations."

"Yeah, no," I say, slightly annoyed at the interruption. "We'll be fine. Direct route, please."

He rolls his eyes again and mutters something under his breath about that being bullshit and how we'll see that he was right. I can only imagine the crap he hears. I doubt I'll come close to some of the stories he's listened to or anything he's witnessed people doing in his backseat, but for me, this is a lot. It's a shameful past that I'm not entirely ready to share, but have to regardless. If I want something serious to happen between us, she deserves to know the real me with all the tainted pieces hidden just below the surface.

To her credit, Jessi's all ears. The story has to begin years ago? She doesn't care. She's here for it. Leg up on the seat to better face me, eyes trained on mine, and one hand nervously fidgeting with that loose thread from her shorts.

I tell her how my aunt married someone rich, became a super-wealthy widower, and then when she died, she left all of it to my parents and their children. I explain how Calista already had plans for her studio and used the inheritance money to buy a condo and get her business started, while I somewhat squandered mine. Once I hit 18, I blew it all on college for a history degree I'll never use and various trips to historical places–all part of my well-rounded education; at least that's what I told myself. I don't have quite as many regrets about that one, but now that I'm sharing an apartment with two roommates, I admit I'm more than jealous of Calista's living arrangements.

"Part of that jealousy," I say, psyching myself up for the tough parts ahead, "is why I wasn't always an exemplary employee at the studio. By my senior year of college, I was broke and working part time for Calista doing mostly tech work while occasionally filling in for a class here and there when they were desperate. By then, I'd gotten used to my cushy life-style of sushi for lunch each day and eating out each night for dinner. I needed to make more money, and fast."

Jessi's face is almost unreadable, aside from a slight upturn of her lips. A bit of encouragement for me to keep going. The cab driver's eyes glance back from time to time using the rearview mirror. Is it strange I don't want to let him down with my story?

"So anyway," I continue, ready to tackle the worst parts. "A few friends and I came up with this idea to use the studio as a secret party location. Everything about it was perfect for small gatherings of college students. We charged an afford-able entrance fee and had kegs for all-you-can-drink beer. No DJ to hire. We did that ourselves with our phones since the rooms were already set up for music with the speaker systems. Then it evolved to around-the-world parties where different rooms had different themes... We went all out some nights."

"Until Sonya caught you?" Jessi asks, again mostly neutral with her expression, but there was a hint of empathy there, too.

The driver shook his head, unimpressed with my revelation.

"She left her phone at work. She called the studio's land line on the off-chance someone was here and would pick up. Sure enough, some asshole answered the desk phone with a few choice words. She told me later she heard my voice in the background, otherwise she would have called Calista or the cops right away."

We're on the bridge going over the East River. I need to wrap this up and not ask for a few extra laps around the block. I don't want to give him the satisfaction.

"Sonya shows up, figures out we're letting people in the back entrance, easily gains entry to the studio, and finds me in the upstairs office off the back hallway."

This gets a chuckle out of Jessi, and I'm relieved. I was quite the womanizer back in the day, but now I'm nothing like the man I was in college. I hope she can see that.

"You're telling me tonight wasn't the first time Sonya caught you in the studio with a half-naked woman?"

I sigh. "Unfortunately, no. But I was more concerned about Sonya telling Calista about the parties than the sex in the studio stuff."

At the word "sex" the driver's eyes dart once again to the back seat and I stare him down as I say, "The sex stuff wasn't the issue. That's not what we're discussing. Eyes on the road. Please."

More muffled laughter from Jessi as the driver shrugs it off, mumbling about how the story would be a whole lot better if it had been about the sex stuff.

"Long story short–"

The driver huffs in disagreement; I ignore him.

"Sonya gave me the lecture of a lifetime and I came to some hard conclusions that night. I stopped with the parties and stuff, and right after graduation, I started working as a legit instructor and tech guy almost immediately. Sonya never mentioned it again to me, and she never held it over my head. Until a few months back."

"We're coming up to your stop, or I can detour," the driver offers, a smug quality to his voice as he waits, expecting me to request a few extra laps to buy more time.

"We're fine. I'm almost done."

Jessi can't hide her amusement at my annoyance with the driver. If only she knew how cute she is when she's trying to suppress a grin or a bit of laughter. I push the adorableness of her from my mind. I need to get this out and be done with it.

"Sonya asked me to help her. Her son's having health issues and some would-be clients asked for later class times. They couldn't make it in for lessons until well after the 9:30 class. She saw an opportunity to do a bit of side-hustling by teaching a late class and pocketing all the cash. All of it going to medical bills."

"What did she need your help with?"

"The cameras, access to the building. That sort of thing."

"She needed your help to keep it a secret from your sister?"

The word "sister" is a knife to the chest. Or maybe I should say a knife to the back, since that's what I'm doing to Calista, stabbing her in the back. But Calista is financially stable; Sonya is not. The arrangement can't be hurting Calista's bottom line too much if she hasn't noticed, and she's opening a second location.

"Sonya was struggling; Calista was... Not quite herself. She hasn't been lately for some reason. I felt like I owed it to Sonya. It's not like she gave me an ultimatum or even brought up what happened all those years ago, but it was in the air around us. I needed to pay her back, and I did. With my silence."

"And we're here," the driver says as we pull up to the curb. "You know, you can always finish your conversation in her apartment. That's where we are, right? Your place?"

Put on the spot, Jessi's caught off guard, almost as much as I am. Who the fuck is this guy? His arm is around the back of the passenger seat headrest so he can turn to see us.

"I've got it," I tell Jessi, already armed with my credit card and swiping it through the machine.

"Did you want to come up?" she asks me. The door is still open, and she's standing on the sidewalk, the sweetest smile on her face that almost convinces me to say yes. To always say yes to this woman.

"I should probably get back."

The driver is appalled, shaking his head in disbelief and turning back to the street.

"It's been a night," I continue, "and I need to figure some things out."

"Right. That was a lot. You're working tomorrow?"

"Yeah, I'll see you then."

Jessi shuts the door, and I give the driver my address, but he doesn't move. Instead, he says, "I'm waiting for the lovely lady to get into her apartment building since you refused to exit the vehicle."

"What the hell is your problem? 99% of the drivers don't say shit to me. Tonight, of all nights, I get stuck with you."

"Because you're lucky," he insists, pulling away from the curb before I have a chance to jump out. "Between a thirty-year career as a psychiatrist and now three years as a driver, I know everything. I've heard and seen it all."

I don't respond. I meant it when I said I had stuff to figure out and the last thing I need right now is some random stranger getting involved in something he knows nothing about.

"Like that, there? She wanted you to come up. Society won't let her beg, but damn did she want you to, and you just blew her off. You're going to see her at work tomorrow? You better show up with her favorite drink or flowers or something. Otherwise, she's going to think you're not interested."

"She'd never think that." I hate that I'm engaging, but I feel the overwhelming need to put this jackass in his place. We've had a million little moments together and the chemistry between us is undeniable. It's not possible she can misread this single, minor incident as me not being interested. I feel for the three decades' worth of clients who potentially followed his every word of advice.

"There's a saying: If he wanted to, he'd do it. Have you heard that saying before?"

I reluctantly shake my head. I should probably verbalize responses so he keeps his eyes on the road, but I'm annoyed and sometimes when I'm annoyed I get petty.

"Well, *she's* heard of it. Her friends are probably in a group FaceTime session right now telling her how you're not interested, because if you wanted to go up and have sex with her, you would have. Just like you broke into your employer's office to have sex with those women. You wanted to, and so you did."

"That's not what–"

"Tomorrow, you need to do something that separates you from a person who isn't interested in her. Court her. What's her favorite candy? Buy a pack on the way to work. Trust me."

I'm still in my petty phase. I don't show any signs that I agree with him, even though mentally I do.

"Yeah," I eventually mutter as we cross back over the bridge and head north towards my apartment in Washington Heights.

"Good. Now, let's discuss what's going on between you and your sister."

CHAPTER 15
ANNA, SUNDAY, JULY 14TH

"You're here early," I say to Luke when I walk into work the next day and see him behind the counter with Florence. "Have some tech work to do?"

"Always. Updating the website calendars and events is never ending. I could probably do it from home, but every time I try something comes up that I need a specific picture of the studio or information that's on the computer files rather than the cloud. That sort of thing, so I just come in whenever I need to work on it."

Damn. I was kidding. I thought he was here early to see me. I have to remind myself that Luke is in his twenties. Not even in his late twenties. This is what guys do at that age. They flirt with and try to sleep with everyone. When they lose interest in one woman or when things get too complicated (e.g., last night's debacle), they move on to someone else.

I can't believe I invited him up to my apartment last night. When was the last time I've had someone besides Paige up there? I can't even say; I never invite people up. And I wouldn't have done it last night except the cab driver put the idea out there and our conversation was flowing and moving back into lighter territory.

Ugh. What the fuck was I thinking? As soon as I got up to my floor, there was Paige with a bag of takeout in the hallway, chatting up the DoorDash woman. How would I have explained that to Luke?

Since she had takeout and I had updates, we ate and talked for a little over an hour last night, analyzing the situation. Paige said that he probably wasn't all that interested because if he wanted to come up, he would have. Some sort of TikTok advice she'd been seeing, reminiscent of the early 2000s when women all read that book *He's Just Not That Into You* and repeated the title to each other any time a man threw any sort of red flag in the commitment department. According to her, if he wanted to, he would have. Since he didn't come up, he didn't want to. I reminded her of all the internal conflicts he was juggling, and she shook her head. "He's in his sexual prime. Early twenties. You don't remember college guys because it's been so long. I promise you, I'm right. He's adorable and a great guy, but he's probably not dating material. Not for another five to ten years, at least. Sorry, babe, but better you know now than later, right?"

I'd agreed with her last night, popped a gummy before bed, and promised myself I'd put it out of my mind. Clearly I was already high when I'd made that promise because here I am at the desk, all googly eyes over Luke being here.

He licks his lips and cracks a smile before setting a frosted doughnut on a little plate and a coffee from our coffee shop up on the counter.

"I also wanted to be in the studio first thing so I could give you these."

It's been ages since I've felt butterflies in my stomach over a guy. A woman could really get used to this–a man who exceeds expectations and refuses to fall into the stereotypes of what I think of as the average man. Why had I been so quick to write him off over one simple gesture last night? Was I the immature one?

"Is it maple?" I ask, though I'd bet my life it is since he already knows it's my favorite.

"Maple," he confirms, our eyes playing a game of chicken, neither of us willing to look away. With a majority of my attention focused on Luke, I am still painfully aware of Florence in my periphery, taking it all in as she pretends to type something into a document.

"And I thought maybe I could get a bit of advice from you while you get set up for class?"

After a quick sip, I store the doughnut and coffee behind the counter for later. "Ask away," I say, as I lead us back into the studio. Florence watches us walk away. Calista should have had Florence on her payroll as a spy. She misses nothing. Maybe she does have her on spy payroll. Maybe she's already texting Calista now that Luke brought me gifts and we're alone in the back studio. Fuck it. That's all explainable; perfectly reasonable actions for coworkers.

We're in the same studio where we almost had hot sex in front of all the floor-to-ceiling mirrors. That's not a possibility now because I have a class coming in mere minutes, but it does give me a slight pause. There have been a few times since where we almost kissed. Like at the counter over the gifted doughnut. Aside from Florence eyeing us up, every other aspect of the moment was kiss-worthy: the light romantic music in the background, his fingers on the counter brushing up against mine with a suggestive stroke of one of his against mine, and the way when his eyes finally did break from mine, it was only to look down at my lips.

Florence and Calista act as a brick wall against any romantic advances. Mainly Calista. Though even that barrier is quickly crumbling. I texted her two days ago saying I had information for her and she hasn't texted back. Nothing. It's un-freaking real. The woman throws thousands at me, concocts this crazy scheme, and then doesn't answer back? It makes no sense.

The more I think about it, and I did think about it for half of the night last night after I banned romantic ideas of Luke from my mind, the more I keep coming to the same conclusion. I need to come clean to Luke about everything and work with him to figure out what's really going on with Calista. To get her the help she may need, because day by day this is turning more and more into a "blink if you need help" type of situation. As her brother Luke should know if something might be up.

Besides, I don't know how much longer I can keep not kissing him, and I know he's suffering from the same affliction. I glanced over my shoulder on the way into the studio and caught him staring at my ass as I walked. Granted, I was giving a quick show, hence the sneaky look over the shoulder to make sure it was working.

"Gabe's sealed himself off from the rest of the world today to get through the final five hours of the fairy smut audiobook," Luke says. We both grab rags to wipe down the poles before a new group of students floods in.

"That's... impressive. Does he actually like the book or just the woman?" We start at poles on opposite ends of the room; we'll meet in the middle when we're finished.

Luke laughs. "Both. Gabe's on the brink of cult membership with this book. It's 36 hours long on audio. He's listening at two times the speed just to get through it. He's joined a Discord Server, and he's sucked Trav in."

I mock gasp. "*You're* the only one missing out on Magnus's magnum fairy cock?"

His eyes widen. "You too?"

I can't keep a straight face around Luke to save my life, so I immediately cave and let out a laugh as I shake my head. "When you first mentioned it the other day, I was intrigued and Googled the title. I like historical fiction best, though I'm not above some added smut." I intentionally say all of that right as I'm cleaning off my last pole, my hand expertly stroking up and down with the rag.

Luke's final pole is thoroughly cleaned as well, but he continues to stroke as he says, "I can see the appeal. Gabe's been reading out some of the extra spicy parts to us. I didn't hate it."

The thought of these grown men having a read-aloud with fairy porn makes me laugh. "Sounds like a regular literary frat house."

"It is, which is why I'm here asking you for advice. The frat brothers and I are clueless about how Gabe should approach this. Trav says Gabe should go all out: pages of notes, comments on every topic they bring up, and so on, while I'm telling him to pull way back. To not come on too strong. But all of our advice is coming from two guys who have never been to a book club meeting. Ever. Much less a book club meeting slash date, if that's what this is."

"What makes you think I've had book club dates?"

He gives me a look, one eyebrow arched high enough to dare me to say I haven't been to a book club meeting or dated someone in my book club.

"Okay, fine. I've been in a few book clubs in my lifetime." The phrase gives me a moment's pause, a reminder that my lifetime, especially my time as an adult, has been significantly longer than his.

"See? I knew it," he says, oblivious or unconcerned about the different lengths of our lifetimes. "How should he play it? How would *you* play it?"

I relinquish the pole, and we both throw our rags into the bin. I have one minute before I need to let my students in for their lesson.

"He needs to win over the other club members. He *cannot* mansplain *anything,* and as the newest member, he probably shouldn't dominate the conversation, no matter how much he knows his shit. Tell him to buy a few apps for the table as a thank you for letting him join at the last minute and to keep up with the conversation, but hold back until he understands the flow of the group."

Luke grins back at me, nodding a universal understanding of what I've said. "Free food. Why didn't I think of that?"

"Maybe you're not as smart as you think you are, Luke Pluto." My bedroom voice is coming out, a knee-jerk reaction thanks to my proximity to him and our current location. This room, Studio B, now does something to me. There are memories forever seared into my mind; memories that make my body respond regardless of the fact that this thing with Luke can only be temporary. Once he knows the truth, that I've been lying to him and everyone else for almost a month now, it's highly likely that I'll lose him, and all of this, forever.

"Is food the way to your heart?" Luke asks, looking thoroughly pleased with himself having just given me that delicious-looking maple frosted doughnut. We're right at the closed door separating us from twelve eager pole students. There isn't too much of a height difference between us, so we're almost eye-to-eye and mouth-to-mouth. I open the door before I'm too tempted to start something there isn't nearly enough time to finish.

He laughs, aware of what he's doing to me; knowing that this action is a defense mechanism.

"Food is the way to everyone's heart. Am I right?" The adult students nod enthusiastically, some verbalizing their favorite dishes and ways their significant others have forever solidified their love with some surprise meal, snack, or treat over the years. I give myself a few seconds to relish in the safety of this space where people of all sizes freely talk about their love of all things food without feeling shame or the need to justify their taste in unhealthy food with how they also eat homemade kale chips or do shots of apple cider vinegar. Then I need to shut down those thoughts because I'm *not* home here at the studio. I'm a temporary resident and it's not healthy mentally for me to even pretend otherwise.

"Partner up and grab a pole. We'll get started as soon as Luke vacates the room," I say loud enough for the class to hear, but I'm only speaking to him.

He puts his hands up in surrender. I notice in my periphery half the class is getting ready and the other half is blatantly watching the show Luke and I are putting on. The will-they-won't-they vibes we're flooding throughout the room.

"I have my pole strength classes Tuesday night. I wouldn't hate it if you stopped by," he says before slipping out of the door.

CHAPTER 16
LUKE, TUESDAY, JULY 16TH

"Have you seen Calista lately?" I ask Florence. The classes we have here are often sporadic with their times and who is teaching them. Instructors are coming and going at odd hours and on different days. But Florence is the sun and moon of the studio. She's the only one with set hours and the only one that isn't holed up in some back room for most of the time they're at work.

In short, if someone had seen Calista at work the past few weeks, it would have been her.

"Not since she hired Jessi," Florence answers without consulting any calendars or taking a moment to give it thought.

"Are you sure? That was weeks ago."

Florence does not appreciate being questioned, and she gives me a look to make sure I know it.

"She was here the night before setting up Jessi in the system, and I haven't seen her since. Yeah, I'm sure. It was memorable."

Jessi comes into the studio, dressed for class and looking pleasantly surprised to find me at the front desk. "Hey! I was going to do a bit of free pole before your class at seven."

I will never tire of that smile. Sometimes, a group of us will be at the desk between classes, and now and then I'll look up and see her beaming at me. Smiling with her entire face, especially her eyes, which I could get lost in all night. This is the smile she's giving me now.

At the sight of Jessi and me together, Florence stops her typing and grabs her drink. She leans back into her seat and eyes us expectantly. I rarely give a fuck what people at the studio think about my love life, but my irritation with Calista is spreading to everyone around me, so I jerk my head for Jessi to follow me and we head up to the tiny office upstairs.

"My class got canceled. Let's talk upstairs."

"Is this about Calista?" Jessi asks when we're halfway up and out of earshot of the others.

I stop in my tracks and look over my shoulder. "What did you hear?"

Her head and upper body ease back. "I haven't... I'm going off what you said before. In the cab."

I'm relieved to hear there isn't more craziness to the story, but I wish there was, since the story I currently have makes very little sense to me.

"Have a seat," I say, pulling out the rolling desk chair as far as the wall behind me will allow. Calista refused to use one of the actual office rooms as an office because she found she could fit a few poles in it. Instead, she converted this closet into an office. Though by city standards, I supposed it's almost spacious.

She sits but still gives me enough room to access the laptop. While I'm typing, she's checking out the decor: a small succulent in a pot painted to look like Leslie Knope's face, a daily quotes calendar that's stuck in April, and a hanging photo of Calista cutting the ribbon at the studio opening along with the first dollar she made. I'm in the photo, too, but I'm seventeen and pissed off. She'd chosen the same day as my high school graduation as her opening day.

Which was more exciting for my parents: Calista opening her own business or me graduating high school?

I hope Jessi doesn't notice. Petty is not a good look on me, and I don't need anything reminding her about our age difference. I've already noticed the occasional age gap reference and the quick look of shock that ripples over her features. It's gone shortly after, but I'd rather not push that particular button if I don't have to.

"I haven't seen Calista since before you were hired," I say, partly to get the conversation going and partly to get her eyes off that photo. "I don't know how I missed it," I explain, still opening up my email because I was distracted by my close proximity to Jessi and that fucking intoxicating scent that I can only pick up on when I'm this close to her. "But it hit me today how long it's been since I've seen her and then just now Florence said she hasn't seen Calista in the studio since the day before your first class."

"That's interesting because Paige–" Jessi pauses.

"Paige? Calista's old college roommate, Paige?"

"Oh, no. Sorry," she stammers, embarrassed at having sparked my interest only to let me down. "I was just going to say that page, the webpage you just had open. One of the ads was one that I keep seeing, too. Looks like we're on the same algorithms." She gives me a weak smile. "Sorry. Totally off topic and not at all important right now."

I don't comment because I have no idea what to say. Florence put ideas in my head about Jessi having secrets or acting weird, and now I'm also paranoid about Calista. Am I over-reaching and looking for things that aren't there?

"Is this what you wanted to show me?"

She's pointing to an image of our biggest local competition, Pole Life. It is what I wanted to show her, but I had also wanted to get her opinion on why Calista hasn't been to the studio in so long, why she's acting so sporadic lately with responses to calls and texts, why she sent me a link to this

TikTok account of our competitors, and why all of this was done through email, text, and Florence because we haven't properly spoken in forever.

"Yeah," I say softly, feeling a sense of defeat when I don't say any of the other stuff, and the moment passes us by. "Calista sent it over earlier. I think she wants to make sure I know what I'm up against, and I wanted to get your opinion."

I hit play on the video and turn up the volume. Once the camera pans away from the logo on the front wall and goes into one of the studio rooms, Jessi leans forward, her eyes focused on the screen.

"Damn," she says, her voice denoting a feeling of complete awe at what she is witnessing. "That might be the most beautiful couple I have ever seen. Ever."

She's not wrong. The woman reminds me of Nicole Kidman with her rich, long red hair, and the man looks like Ryan Gosling but somehow more good-looking, though I can't really place why. Maybe the chiseled features? I don't know. I admittedly don't pay much attention to him whenever she's on the screen.

"Are they together?" she asks, seeing her give him a quick ass grab right before he hops on the pole.

"Yeah, they're married. Opened the studio together a year or so after Calista did. She's always said they were her biggest competition. They have four locations now, which might explain why she's been out of the studio lately, working to open up Art of Spinning's second location."

We're silent as we both watch the video. I've seen it a few times now. He, Marco, is announcing that he'll be at Pole Masters this weekend and he's giving a quick preview of his moves on the pole while she, Maria, does a sultry little dance off to the side and cheers him on. The last bit is promo-based while they go over classes they offer and their special deals for new clients.

When the spell is broken and Jessi can turn her eyes away

from Marco, she scoffs. "It only has a few dozen views. *This* is what Calista is all wound up about?"

"It's not about the TikTok account. One of the sole reasons I was doing the competition was to get the word out about our studio. It's practically a moot point now that I'm up against Marco, Mr. Sexual Stud on a Pole."

Her eyes widen. "You're clearly having a day, so I'm going to disregard that last comment."

"I can't tell you how much I appreciate that." Mr. Sexual Stud was not my finest moment, and as flustered as I am with everything going on, the last thing I need is to be making embarrassing comments while Marco continues to display his sexual prowess via his expert pole moves.

The video is on replay and we stare at the movements on the screen while my mind tries to sort through everything. I was finally making a name for myself, bringing my own students in through word of mouth of my current students and small paper ads I've placed in all the local establishments that will let me. Going up against Marco and having Calista calling me out, saying she already knows I can't beat him... It's all such a blow to my ego.

"Hey," Jessi says, placing her hand on mine, her thumb softly stroking between my thumb and finger, guiding my mind back to the present and away from my jumbled thoughts. "Are you okay?"

I don't answer. I don't want to lie, but I also don't want to get into everything right now.

Jessi stands and turns to face me, her stomach against mine in the cramped office. She's leaning back ever so slightly to give me space, or to get a better look at me as her eyes search mine, trying to find the source of what's bothering me besides the obvious.

When I confronted Calista via email about not being present in the studio anymore, she turned it around on me. How there are a million things she needs to do to open a new location, and how I've been here for years now. As a long-time employee and as part of the family, I should be able to run everything in her place. She'd worded her email much nicer than that, but I had trouble eliminating her snarky voice in my mind as I read and reread it.

Well then, if I'm in charge now, I guess that means I get to change up the rules. Starting with the one that prohibits me from what I'm about to do.

CHAPTER 17
ANNA, TUESDAY, JULY 16TH

'm going to tell him. I want to tell him everything. All of it. The only reason I don't is because I'm waiting to hear from Calista. She has a lot going on right now and it's only fair I give her another day to get back to me. At the very least, I feel like I should wait until after the competition since I know she'll be there. What I need to say is more of a face-to-face conversation rather than a text, anyway.

So instead of telling him about how I really do know Paige and how that connection led me to this ridiculous predicament, I cup his jaw with my hand. Unable to stop my thumb, I gently work his cheek, as if trying to wipe away the look of worry spreading across his face.

He leans into my hand, his lips grazing the pad of my thumb, and I think we both know there's only one direction this can go.

Just like he's leaning into my hand, I'm going to lean into my character a tiny while longer. Technically, Jessi exists. I am her. My past is a splattering of lies, but the woman he's gotten to know this summer has mostly been me. Regardless of what he calls me, it's me he's kissing and touching and wanting with an unyielding, fiery desire in his eyes.

Those same eyes, already hooded with need, are locked in on my lips. I'm leaning back against the desk and slightly shorter than he is. With a tiniest tip of my chin upwards, he lowers his, and finally he melts every part of me with the softest of kisses. With our lips pressed together, my lower one nestling in between his as if it was always meant to be there, we say all the things that we can't verbalize to each other. I know there's more going on with him than what he's telling me, and he knows I have secrets of my own.

Instead, with this softest of soft kisses, we tell each other that it's okay. As we lean in and deepen the kiss ever so slightly, we tell each other that we know enough, for now. His fingers comb through my hair and he gives a gentle tug at the nape, saying that we can do this anyway, be deeply intimate in a way we both so desperately want to, even with all the unknowns between us.

Then I make the mistake of breathing in his addictive scent right in the middle of the sweet, sweet kiss, and suddenly it's not so innocent anymore. He and I deepen the kiss together, already completely in sync, or maybe it just feels that way.

There's no room in the closet office and that suits us perfectly. The door is already closed so we can both fit, and no one ever comes in here except Luke and Calista. There isn't a class starting in a few minutes, and Florence isn't side-eying us. We're just two consenting adults who have been eye fucking each other for weeks, but now we've finally found ourselves in the perfect circumstances to do something about it.

His hands are moving behind me. Doing what? I couldn't say because I'm all in with what's happening with our kiss and with his mouth as he makes a trail to my neck and collar. My focus is on the debilitating sensation of pleasure mixed with pain when he bites on my shoulder. He kisses where he bit and whispers in my ear, "Was that okay?"

"Yes," I whimper back. "More." This is the way we reveal ourselves to one another. There are some things we aren't willing to say yet, but here in this situation, maybe we can both let it all ride, consequences be damned. It's refreshing. Lately, I rarely find myself in bed with anyone under thirty. I've had one too many instances of a man who doesn't fully understand how to please a woman, how to make sex good for all parties involved. Luke taking the lead and then confirming that I too am into it? That's hot as fuck.

"You like it a little rough?" he asks, his head now buried in my neck enough that I can feel the five-o'clock-shadow he's got going on. Invisible the naked eye, but there according to my delicate skin.

"Yes." His rough skin on my neck and his gentle hair pulls? I'm here for it all.

"You'll tell me if I'm too rough?"

This isn't performative. Much to my chagrin, he pulls his face out of my neck to look me in the eye for my response.

"Yes. Promise," I say before shoving his lips back to where I so desperately need them.

This was a great idea. In my current state of pure desire, I'm 100% sure that this bonding, which includes a fair amount of vulnerability on both sides, is better than anything we could have achieved through conversation.

Speaking of bonding and vulnerability, I wonder if he's ever had his nipples played with before. I'm guessing probably not. Some guys are all about it, possibly even more than I enjoy having my own nipples sucked, licked, and pinched. And some guys hate it. Based on everything I've seen about Luke so far, I'm willing to bet he's at least a little bit of a nipples guy, and this feels like the right time to find out.

While he's been devouring me, my fingers have been working the buttons on his shirt and I now have access to those perfect pecs and nipples that are craving my attention. I can tell.

"I'm assuming then that you like it rough, too," I say right as I give those nipples a pinch between my fingers and make the smallest of a circular motion to give them a slight tug.

"Fuck me," he groans into my neck, his cock pressing harder against me, begging for access. I take that as an invitation to duck down to lick and suck each nipple, flicking them with my tongue before ending each mini massage with a kiss.

"You're a nipples guy," I say, pleased with my new information and already thinking of ways I'll put it to use here in the closet and hopefully in other places in the near future.

"I am now." With one hand he holds my face and claims my mouth again, eager for more deep kisses that leave us both breathless. As we kiss, he uses his palm to smack my ass cheek–somewhat on the side given our cramped quarters–with the perfect amount of pressure that sends more building heat between my legs. The temperature of that area quickly increasing to scorching levels.

"I've been dreaming of this firm ass since the first day I saw you," he practically growls. He gives an appreciative squeeze before using both hands to hoist me up onto the desk. Sneaky little fucker must have been clearing it off before.

With me now sitting on the edge of the desk, he effortlessly spreads my legs and steps between them. I feel every inch of his hard length rubbing up against me since the material of our clothing is so thin. He shifts his waist and I groan into our kiss. The friction feels so good, but it isn't nearly enough.

There's been a build-up for weeks now with stolen glances and blatant stares alike, flirty conversations via text and in person, and that one time I taught him to be a stripper as we danced and shed clothing together in the studio. The anticipation might actually overtake me if there are any interruptions this time.

All signs from Luke say that feeling is mutual.

We're back to intimate, get-to-know-you kissing while I grip his ass and pull him closer, encouraging him to grind up against me like we're teenagers dry humping the night away.

"We should probably talk at some point," he says, his voice husky and breathy.

"Yeah. At some point," I agree, hoping he doesn't mean any time soon. Because what we're doing right now is a damn good deep dive into our personality and preferences. I know he enjoys giving and receiving nipple play, I know his cock is probably a shower which is perfect because I already have a decent outline view of it and much bigger than that might be too much for me, and he's about to learn that while I trim it up down there, I like to keep my hair just as Mother Nature intended.

"Soon," I hastily add, worried that his brain is about to kick in and put an end to it all before we get to the best parts.

"Okay," he agrees, "soon." Then his finger traces down the strap of my top, over the hump of my breast, and lands on the fabric between before hooking and pulling the elastic material to the side, letting my boob pop out. He repeats the act on the other side to balance things out.

"Beautiful." Luke licks his lips as he admires me. "Absolutely stunning tits." I couldn't agree more. It's one of my favorite things about my body and it's a good sign that he's a boob man since I've got a fabulous rack. He works his thumbs over my peaked nipples, similar to the way I handled his, complete with the pinch and roll and I'm near ready to explode at this point. I am on fire and this thing we're doing with his clothed cock against my clothed pussy isn't cutting it.

"Be patient." He says more to my boobs than to me since his face is still buried in them. "I'll get there."

At this point, I'm slightly freaked out that he is somehow actually in my mind. "I'm patient," I pant back. Lies. Just like when I'm reading and I rush through the book only to be disappointed that it's over, I sometimes get too antsy during the foreplay and rush towards the main event. Most guys don't notice; they're happy to rush along with me. Luke is not most guys.

At this, he pauses and looks up at me, an accusing half-smile on his face. "You're adorable when you try to lie."

I'm so startled by the word, my sex-addled brain can't respond. Lucky for me, he's already on to something else, the comment dropping from his mind as soon as he said it.

Luke moves the chair in front of me and takes a seat. This man intends to spend some serious time down below, enough to warrant the use of a chair.

His powerful hands grip my shapely gams, digging in for a deep message, then he spreads my legs enough for his head to fit between my dancer's muscled thighs. Before I can react, he carefully bites the fabric of my bottoms and gives a quick, brutish tug. Fabric still between his teeth, he looks up at me, and I know this image of him right as he is now will make several appearances in my upcoming fantasies. I would never have requested someone bite at the thin fabric covering my most delicate of areas, but now that it's happened, I can't un-experience it and would never want to.

He lets go, and it snaps back into place.

"Those need to go. I want full access to that pussy."

He leans back as I close my legs and lift myself a few inches off the desk. With ease, he slips them off, then places his hands on my knees to open me to him once again. I swear he almost whimpers at the sight. I expect him to kiss a line up my thigh again, or tease his way in there, but it turns out he is indeed just as inpatient as I am.

"Stunning," he's able to say right before his fingers are spreading me open and making way for his tongue, just to the side of my clit.

I was wrong before. I had thought that the sight of him, looking up at me with fabric clenched in his teeth, was the hottest thing I'd see in our closet meet up, but this moment is clearly taking over. He adjusts his hands to find the perfect position and settles his palms on the upper part of my thigh. His thumbs hold me open while he tastes every inch of me.

"You are drenched," he says, muffled against me, the vibration from his voice adding a pleasant sensation to an already toe-curling experience.

"You have that effect on me." I lean back against the wall and rest my legs on his shoulders so they dangle down his back. While he works at building up my release, I rake my fingernails through his hair, occasionally guiding him on his mission.

We hear footsteps outside of the office and I immediately freeze. Someone is either about to turn the doorknob and find the door mysteriously locked, even though it never is, or someone needs a random item from the supply closet next door.

Fuuuuuck.

We hear the muffled voices of multiple people outside the office door. How many? It could be dozens. After we were caught by Sonya, my mind only imagines the worst: an entire class somehow needing to all cram into the office even though there's no possible way. Physics and logic would never allow it, but still my mind, in its current state of panic, is sure that's what's about to happen. My legs clamp around Luke's head, and I hold my breath.

And Luke? That kinky bastard doesn't even flinch. I'm on the brink of orgasming with what could be a pack of nuns on the other side of the door for all we know, and he decides that now is the best time to slip in a finger—nay, two fingers—and start that come hither motion with his digits while his tongue hits my ready and eager clit.

Eyes wide, I look down at him, only to find him completely immersed in the task at hand.

Okay, so we're doing this.

The voices continue outside, but I'm not worried about who it is and what they're saying. Instead, I embrace it the way Luke is. The whole "will someone catch Luke massaging my clit with his tongue" thing is pretty freaking hot. Yes, the door is locked, but who knows who has a key. Calista is unhinged; she could barge in at any minute.

"Luke," I whimper as loud as I dare. His hand still in place and massaging away, he pulls his face back just enough that I can see his glistening jaw.

Fuck me. Now, I mouth since I don't dare let out a sound. I have very little control over my body. Every part of me is begging for the orgasm I'm so close to achieving.

He licks me off his lips and gives a devilish grin. Then he reaches into one of the desk drawers and pulls out a condom from a stash of hot pink foil with the words "Here Cums the Bride" on them.

Once he's covered, Luke stands and I wrap my legs around his waist so his tip is right at my entrance, and then he leans forward and his mouth is against my ear. He flicks my lobe with his tongue and whispers, "I'll make you come, but you have to do it quietly."

He inches his hips forward, but still only the tip is inside me. I push my heels into his lower back and the tops of his firm ass, but he doesn't budge.

"You have to promise," he says into my ear.

"I promise." My voice is soft and breathy and desperate.

"Good girl."

Good girl? Not only do I have some kind of weird glasses kink, but now I'm also the kind of woman who gets off to "good girl"?

Yes. Yes, I am. Thanks to the hours of foreplay in the weeks leading up to tonight and the magical tongue work and voyeurism happening in the office, it takes me mere minutes to come apart once Luke slides that perfect, hot-pink covered cock into me.

I can feel my nails digging into his skin as I do everything I can to not make a sound. For fuck's sake, what the hell are those people still doing outside the office?!

"Don't worry about them," he says, sensing my inability to completely let go while there's an unknown audience a few feet away. "Focus on me, on us."

He cups my chin and guides my face so that our noses are touching, our eyes concentrated on each other in this intense, vulnerable moment. Nowhere to hide; no way to hold back.

We kiss. Deep, sensual, probably considered sloppy under normal circumstances, but when inhibitions are already out the door and the animal instincts kick in, no one cares. He bites my lip and tugs as he pulls away.

"Jessi," he pants soft enough so that only I can hear. It might have broken my heart if I hadn't already been lost in my orgasm and the pure bliss that immediately follows primal, urgent sex.

Maybe tomorrow, maybe in a few hours, maybe even in a few minutes, I might feel differently. But for now, I bask in the smell of him as his head slumps down to my shoulder, his body relaxing into mine as he comes down from his own climax. I kiss his neck and shoulders as I take in his scent. I want all the senses burned into my memory.

CHAPTER 18
LUKE, FRIDAY, JULY 26TH

"That's a poor man's date," Trav critiques.

"I'm poor." It was difficult for me to say that in the past. I don't dare tell anyone this because it comes off as, and is, incredibly insensitive, but people don't realize how hard it is to go from having money to not having money. My family did okay growing up. We had everything we needed. There were annual vacations, food on the table, and the occasional splurges. But there also weren't trips to Europe, I was frequently told, "We have food at home," and most of my wardrobe came from the sale racks or my own paychecks from after-school jobs.

That might be why I lost my ever-loving mind in college when I finally had access to Aunt Lonnie's inheritance. My parents invested in real estate–a Painted Lady in Cape May– and my sister invested in her condo and business. I invested in college. My entire admission, boarding, food, and books all paid for.

Things went south when I got used to having never-ending funds at my disposal. Joining an expensive frat and then getting trashed and booking a trip to Boston for a group of frat brothers–don't worry, boys, it's on me–wasn't seen as a stupid mistake. It was me, living my life to the fullest and spending money on experiences rather than material things. I somehow convinced myself that *I* was better honoring my aunt than the rest of my family members.

The extra money ran out at the end of my junior year of college. So even after I'd graduated and no longer wanted to live in an apartment with a bunch of dudes, I couldn't afford not to. That's when I moved in with Trav and Gabe.

Even though my current situation isn't that far off from how things were before I got the inheritance, I'm still struggling to adjust. There's something about living that way for a few years, and then losing it and knowing it's likely never going to happen again, that makes it that much harder to deal with.

Not that I can complain to anyone about that, ever. I keep it to myself and try to limit my bitterness, especially since it was all my doing.

"You're not *that* poor, are you?" Trav continues, not picking up on any of the hints I'm throwing out.

"It's not just about money. This is what we prefer. I love to cook, she does not, so I'm making us a meal. We both don't want to be around a ton of people like at a restaurant or museum, and we both like being up and moving around. Jessi Googled random places in Central Park that people usually overlook, and it turns out we both haven't been to Shakespeare's Garden yet."

"I think it's supremely romantic. Gabe and I are going to check it out sometime next week," Sasha says, her legs splayed over Gabe's lap as they watch reruns of *The Mindy Project*. Gabe's book club date was a raging success: flirting throughout, a kiss at the end, and plans to meet up every free chance they get. Three dates in and they're already like an old couple in the best ways possible.

"I'll take you right now," Gabe says, cupping her chin and giving her a sweet kiss before leaning back on the sofa. They're not going anywhere. Sasha lives with her parents and three siblings, and Gabe has us. In 30 minutes, they'll have the place to themselves.

"See? Sasha loves it," I say, not caring enough about Trav's criticism to further prove him wrong.

Trav rolls his eyes and gets back to packing. He has a weekend work trip to the Catskills. Everyone in the company was voluntold they're taking a group vacation to improve synergy in the workplace with stronger employee bonds. Or something like that. Corporate work life sounds horrendous.

I double-check everything in the bag: bottles of water; grapes; cheese; and two pesto, tomato, and turkey sandwiches on ciabatta. No actual cooking involved since it's going to be in the upper 80s, but I made the pesto from scratch, so I'm calling it a homemade meal.

"Okay, I'm out of here. Trav, safe travels and good luck surviving an entire weekend with your asshole coworkers."

We fist bump and he gives an appreciative smile. "Don't fuck it up with Jessi."

"Gabe, Sasha," I say, my bag over my shoulder and my hand on the doorknob, "enjoy your night."

"Oh, we will," Sasha said, her voice and facial expression revealing that something was afoot. Probably sex. Good for them.

"First big decision of the day: do we listen to Marcia Gay Harden as she gives us a personal tour?" Jessi says, her thumb hitched over her shoulder to reference the giant sign about the audio tour available.

I blow out a mouthful of air. "That's a tough call. I love Marcia Gay Harden." I mean, who doesn't? But I'd rather not hear her voice today. Jessi and I are outside of the studio together, officially on a date, and the last thing I want is someone else in my ear.

"Such a tough call. I know I'm only familiar with the characters she plays in movies and TV shows, but there's still something about her. For me, it's her humor. She plays this therapist in *First Wives Club*–I died. It's even a kind of cheap slap-stick type of humor, but holy crap does she deliver perfectly. I swear I'm not delusional, but I'm pretty sure we'd be the best of friends if I ever got the chance to meet her. I'm even wearing my best hiking boots today on the off-off-chance that she's here."

Jessi twists on the ball of her foot to give me a better view of her hiking boots and attire. They're worn and her hair is in a large braid that falls over her shoulder. I've been with women before who say they like to go on long walks through the park when it's clearly the first time they've ever been beyond sight of the street, where blisters on their feet and a lack of stamina require us to stop every five to ten minutes to take a break. Jessi is not one of those women.

And that's not to shit on women. I've been the deceitful one on dates, too. Chatting up a lovely woman on the subway, I asked if she wanted to get a drink sometime. She said she was on her way to see some friends at a bar to watch the Nathan's Hot Dog Eating Contest, an annual tradition for them. For no reason beyond wanting to show we had a common interest, I said I love watching that and couldn't believe I forgot it was happening that day. July 4th. It was July 4th, and I pretended I didn't know what day it was. To make matters worse, I ate a giant meal with her and her friends, and then rushed to the bathroom to vomit after watching all of two minutes of the competition. She kindly walked me out of the restaurant, said it was interesting meeting me, and that was the last I saw of her.

I'm thrilled to see Jessi and I are actually compatible and this walk won't end with me giving her a piggyback so her blistered feet don't ache the entire way home. Actually, that sounds mildly delightful. I might just offer one up regardless of how things go.

"Wow, you really are a fan. *First Wives Club*... I don't think I know that one."

Jessi's lips press down, creating a seal as if unwilling to let out what she wants to say.

"I used to watch it on VHS when I was home sick from school. Back in the 90s. Were you, uh, even born then?" Her fingers are fidgeting again. I knew this was coming. At some point, we'd have to acknowledge the obvious age gap between us.

"I should probably come clean," I say, somewhat relieved that this has naturally come up in conversation. "I was wondering about the age, too, so I went into the system and looked up your info, including your birthday."

Her eyes widen ever so slightly and for a moment I think back to what Florence said about being in the witness protection group, but then I remember that's absolute nonsense and Florence is bat-shit crazy.

"You did?" she says, her face once again softening. Maybe she's relieved, too. Rip off the bandage all at once and see if we can stabilize afterwards, or if the damage is beyond triaging and we have to call it.

"Valentine's Day birthday, it's cute. Are you a romantic at heart?" I'm stalling. I'm worried once she hears the actual difference, we won't have any more flirty conversations, and I'm not ready to let those go. There's also a chance we'll never have passionate sex in a closet or anywhere else, and I'm definitely not ready for that reality, either. I don't know that I'll ever be ready.

"More like a few commercial industries have exceedingly taken over my birthday. Not that birthdays were ever big with my family. Holidays weren't a big deal for us."

I give her a few minutes to elaborate, to tell me more

about what Christmas morning was like for her family and how she felt about it, but she doesn't.

"Anyway," she says, officially ending any possibility for further conversation about her family and childhood. "What's the damage? How much are people going to gossip about our age gap?"

"You're basically Leonardo DiCaprio."

Her jaw drops. "I'm going to dump you right before your 30th birthday?"

"Yes, but that means we have six long years together."

Jessi freezes.

"You were born in the 2000s?"

"Barely. January 8, 2000. I'm a little over a week away from being a 1900s baby."

She nods even though she's obviously unconvinced. I don't blame her. I've already had a few conversations with Trav, Gabe, and even Sasha about it. Sasha is seven years older than Gabe. Not quite the same, but helpful nonetheless.

"15 years," she says, her mind likely running through all the scenarios that mine did. When I was this age, she was that age. When I was in this grade, she was this age. Luckily I'm a late oops baby, so I don't need to worry about her being my parents' age or anything creepy like that. Hell, Jessi's the same age as my sister. This is fine.

"Have you said anything to Calista? About us?" she asks, promptly moving on from the age issue.

I wasn't ready for that one. I expected her to want to thoroughly discuss how she was born well into the 20th century while I was on the other side. How she has an actual 9/11 story, while I have no recollection at all. At the very least, I assumed she'd be more concerned about what my parents think rather than Calista.

"No. Just my roommates. And Sasha, Gabe's girlfriend."

Her fingers are a flurry of activity, undoing and redoing her braid.

"Good." She puts her hands in her pockets. "I like your sister. A lot," she adds hastily, "but I figured we could keep this between us until we know for sure what this is?" Her voice hitches at the end, indicating that she's asking a question even though it wasn't worded that way.

"Yeah, of course. Things are kind of strained between Calista and me anyway…"

"Shit. I'm making it worse with—"

"No, it's fine. It was like that before you were hired. It's only gotten worse since, and with Pole Masters tomorrow."

While I'm fumbling about with how difficult things are, Jessi's furrowed brow increases in intensity. "Of course. The competition tomorrow, too. We can go. We should go," Jessi says before I can finish my speech.

This is not what we came to Shakespeare's Garden for. Jessi and I are here for a secluded date, outside the studio and the problems that come with it, and away from our coworkers' prying eyes. To exist without people from work giving us side-glances or people in restaurants asking if we're on a mother-son dinner date.

"No, that's not what I meant by saying all of that. It's just. How did we get from Marcia Gay Harden to this?"

"I don't know." She smiles back at me and the world feels right again. "Want to start over?" She does a little shake of her body, forcing off the bad aura we'd created with our conversation, and I do the same.

"Do you think we should listen to Marcia and take the audio tour?" Jessi asks again, her thumb once more hitched over her shoulder at the green sign at the Shakespeare Garden entrance.

"No, I'd rather walk and talk. You?"

"Same. We'll read a plaque or two as we go."

I hold out my hand. Hers fits perfectly into mine, and we climb the stone stairway surrounded by the old-school wooden fencing.

. . .

The rest of our date is straight out of a cheesy rom-com, complete with Reese Witherspoon. She was wearing big-as-bug-eyes sunglasses and a giant sun hat, but we could tell it was her. We held hands through most of our walk. Jessi and I held hands; Reese was going the opposite direction and did not hold our hands. Our conversation flowed effortlessly as we talked about the garden, Shakespeare, and work. It even dove into the murky waters of politics, which we both survived having similar views on even the most divisive and polarizing issues.

Luckily, that was about the time when we spotted Reese, propelling our conversation back to the lighter topics of favorite movies and television shows.

"I binge watched *Freaks and Geeks*," I say as we go back and forth, listing off our favorites, no matter how obscure, only to find the other is a fan as well. "I had the biggest crush on—"

"Wait, let me guess."

We're sitting in a clearing of sorts. I'm not even sure if we should be off the beaten path like this, but while we were trying to get a better look at a plaque set farther back into the garden, we found a tiny path that led out to a clearing, away from the throngs of people who weren't even supposed to know this place existed. So much for commonly overlooked places in Central Park.

Jessi's sitting cross-legged as we eat, but now her hands are in her lap and regarding me with increased amusement as she pretends to analyze me.

"You're a Kim fan, aren't you? Busy Philipps? The outgoing, rebellious blonde who doesn't care what anyone else thinks. The dangerous one."

I nod my head and heave out an enormous sigh.

"Completely wrong."

"What?" A small chunk of bread fell into her lap earlier, and she takes this moment to chuck it at my face.

I easily lean to my left to dodge the random and uncalled for assault. "It's Linda Cardellini. Lindsay Weir."

Her eyebrows raise in surprise.

"It was always her. Smart and sweet. Innocent."

Jessi rolls her eyes.

"Not like that. I mean innocent in this way that she still saw all the positives of the world. Kim was gorgeous, but jaded."

"Okay, I can see that," Jessi says, licking her lips and taking a sip of water. "Do you want to guess who my *Freaks and Geeks* crush was, over two decades ago when it first aired?"

"I don't have to guess. It was James Franco." I muss up my hair as best I can, so it hangs down and frames my face the way Daniel's did in the show. Then I relax my features and let my eyelids drop a little, like I'm permanently stoned out of mind.

Jessi leans back, her head falling so I can't see her expression beyond the amused look she gave me right before.

"I'm right, aren't I? You're shaking from laughter. I nailed it and you don't know how to defend your crush."

She shakes her head, braid swinging just above the blanket we laid out over the grassy clearing. But instead of sitting back up and debating the merits of James Franco's character like the adults we are, her arms give way and she lays all the way back, still shaking with laughter.

"Lindsay," I say, crawling over to Jessi, so I'm straddling her, my hips above hers, and my hands planted on either side of her head.

"No!" she shrieks back. "No more James Franco impressions." She reaches up and tries to fix my hair, which only results in it getting more messed up. It also results in my skin tingling with the occasional brush of her fingers against my forehead.

When she makes one last ditch effort to tuck a section behind my ear, her fingers trail to the nape of my hair, pulling me down. The laughter is gone.

We kiss on the blanket, the faint sounds of random people and various birds off in the distance, but mostly I'm aware of only the sounds we are making: soft moans and the clink of my buckle as she undoes it. All I can smell is sunscreen, grass, and her.

Looks like we're sex-anywhere-but-the-bedroom type of people. Good to know. Though admittedly I wish I had known sooner. I didn't think to bring condoms to Shakespeare's Garden.

I moan into our kiss as she grips my cock in her hand, her thumb making a circular motion on the tip, spreading around the precum already conjured by this bewitching woman.

"Someone's enjoying the garden," she teases between kisses, her hand still working away, running her fingers up and down the length before showing my balls some love, too.

"Amazing garden. Highly recommend," I say, only half paying attention to the words leaving my mouth because I can't pull my thoughts from–"Holy fuck," I moan, pulling away from our kiss because I can't hold my head up anymore and instead collapse onto my elbows with my forehead resting on the ground above her shoulder.

"Shhh," she chastises. "We weren't the only ones who opted out of the Harden tour. We don't want an audience." She freezes, then her hands are on my chest, pushing me up and to the side so I'm now on my back. "We don't, right? You're not actually an exhibitionist, are you?" Her left eyebrow is raised and her mouth reveals a wicked grin.

"No," I insist, my cock out and at full attention in the middle of a public garden in Central Park.

Unconvinced, she raises her eyebrow a smidge higher.

"You pulled that out." I put my hands up in defense.

"Then I'd better cover it back up."

Jessi leans down, trails her tongue up from my balls to the tip before taking me in her mouth. I bite my lip so I don't cry out. The ticket and potential court date that might result from being caught would suck, but my biggest concern with someone spotting us is having to stop.

CHAPTER 19
ANNA, SATURDAY, JULY 27TH

t's Saturday night and I am with a gaggle of coworkers and pole dancing clients taking up several of the high tops closest to the stage where Luke is about to do a very public strip tease. Aside from Paige, I haven't told anyone about Luke. As I take in the conversation around the table, it doesn't feel like anyone is aware or has suspicions. Except Florence, of course. But I've heard some of her conspiracy theories: Subway makes its sub rolls with old yoga mats, aliens walk among us in disguise, and of course, the Earth is actually flat but appears round in photos because of the curve of the camera lenses. Even if she's said anything to the rest of the staff, there's no guarantee anyone would take stock of her supposed observations.

And Sonya knows, obviously. As far as I can tell, she doesn't know the extent though, and she hasn't said or even hinted anything to me about it since that night. She went right back to her perma-bubbly self.

Tonight I notice she isn't drinking anything. The cover to get into the place is $20 per person and the drinks are beyond pricey. I buy a few pitchers of on-tap beer for the table and insist everyone has a drink on me. A sort of subtle thank you to Sonya for not spilling my secret, and a tiny way to tell all of my coworkers and pole family that I freaking love them to death. I fear literally saying as much would be awkward, so I say it with beer.

Lyric and her husband are here and debating with Mel and her girlfriend about which Netflix series is more binge-able: *Narcos* or *The Diplomat*. The conversation easily pulls everyone into the mix and the table is quickly a buzz with all the safe topics of television, music, and pole dancing outfits and moves.

"Hey, sorry I'm late," Paige says, giving me a quick hug from behind before sliding onto the stool I've been subtly saving for her. I feel Florence's eyes on me and remember too late that even though it makes perfect sense for Paige to be here to support Calista and Luke, it makes no sense at all for her to be hugging me.

"We're not friends. Remember?" I hiss. I'm not annoyed with her; I'm more done with the whole situation. I can't keep anything straight and I'm starting to experience a deep-seated paranoia during each of my conversations, worrying I'm going to say the wrong thing or already have and just haven't realized it yet. My date with Luke went similarly. I had an amazing time, but the shadow of my lies was a permanent haze throughout, ruining what was otherwise a lovely summer day with the sweetest man I've ever met.

"Sorry!" Paige says loud enough for everyone to hear. "I get handsy when I drink and I pregamed earlier."

She shows us her jazz hands as if this is all the proof we need to understand the seemingly inappropriate touching that just went down between us.

"It's okay. We met once or twice," I say, unable to stop perpetuating the lie. "It's not like we're complete strangers."

We carry on this way for a few minutes until I'm sure everyone is so thoroughly bored with our lame conversation that they go back to their own.

It's a Saturday night and with the hour delay to the start of the contest, everyone's been putting back the drinks. The drunk, middle-aged men and women might just revolt if they don't get this thing going soon. Even our table conversation is turning somewhat heated as we've steered into the topic of *Buffy the Vampire Slayer*: the movie versus the television series.

"Where's Calista?" I ask Paige. The table is fully engrossed now in their debate, leaving us to speak quietly but freely.

"No fucking clue." She's surveying the crowd, though I'm not sure if she's looking for Calista, Luke, or someone else entirely.

"You didn't come together?"

She shakes her head. "We were supposed to. I feel bad being annoyed and saying anything shitty about her, but… I think–I don't know what to think. This is beyond Calista's occasional step into erratic behavior. Even for her, this is exceptionally abnormal." It's the cheapest beer they have on tap (I'm back to pinching pennies and can't bring myself to splurge on anything fancier) but she's chugging like she just lost a game of beer pong.

I can tell my brows are furrowed to where I have that deep vertical line between them, but even my vanity can't stop it.

"Luke said something similar the other day," I say, unsure if I'm betraying his trust because we really didn't establish if what was being said was on or off the record. But if anyone deserves to know, I think it's Paige. There's a history there. College roommates sometimes feel like sisters once it's all said and done, and Paige should know Calista's sibling is signaling alerts, too.

Paige nods as she drinks, probably relieved someone else is seeing it as well and can potentially help more than she can.

"I went to her place to pregame a little before coming here," Paige says, mildly out of breath after gulping down the pint in a single, long swig. "Waited and texted outside on the sidewalk since she wasn't answering. The doorman was zero help. Something about the privacy of the occupants."

I pour Paige another beer. I'd be on the floor after a few drinks too quickly on an empty stomach, but I don't have any qualms about Paige's consumption. The woman can drink.

"When I do finally get a text back from her, it's apologetic and about how she forgot, but she'll meet me here."

Every muscle relaxes at that. "Forgetting plans isn't indicative of trouble. She has a lot going on right now."

"No, you don't know Calista like I do. Her mind is a steel fucking trap. She is the original digital planner girl. I can vividly remember her lecturing me about how to set up and use the planner on our BlackBerrys, typing in study sessions, meals, even bathroom breaks during finals cramming sessions. She misses and forgets nothing."

I swirl my straw around in my water, thinking about what Paige is saying and how it's not lining up with what I've seen so far. But then, Calista started her own business and is now looking to expand to another location. A person has to be pretty damn organized to take on and succeed with something like that.

"Anyways," Paige says, finally settling in after drinking a significant portion of her second beer. "I've never been here, and I do not know why. It's full of hot men. Did you know about this?" She holds her pint out, motioning to the plethora of well-dressed, good-looking dudes that almost out-number all the women. She puts it together before I can respond. "Oh, right. They're all gay, aren't they?"

"For tonight's males-only pole dancing competition? It's highly possible. But some might be bi."

Paige raises an interested eyebrow at one of the potentially bi men across the bar, her lips forming a flirtatious smile.

"Indeed. I think I found one already." She gives a quick wink to the hot stranger and then reaches out and places her hand on mine, giving it a quick squeeze. "That's only a minuscule part of why I'm out tonight. I'm here to support you, and Calista if she ever fucking shows up, and little Lukey who turned into a pole dancing savant."

Eventually, our conversation merges with the rest of the pole crew until the music cuts out and the main event is announced with all the fanfare one would expect. Scratch that, mostly what one would expect except for a lone fanatic who thought it would be a good idea to use a whistle as a noisemaker.

"What in the burning pits of hell…" I hear Lyric say as we all turn in our seats to glare at the bonehead sounding a whistle at full blast in a bar. Just as uniformly, our jaws drop at the sight of Calista, blowing and forcing her way through the crowd towards our set of tables, still wearing her sunglasses.

We usher her over and ignore the man on the mic as he covers the rules of how contestants will be scored, and he is happy to ignore us now that we've extracted the whistle from Calista's mouth.

Paige takes Calista's sunglasses and gets off her stool to offer it to the excessively intoxicated woman. "Sit down. Here, have some of Anna's water."

I shoot her a look at the use of my real name around every person in New York who knows me as Jessi, but she's too busy tending to Calista to notice. Likewise, everyone else is focused on Calista, and with all the extra noise and applause, her words don't reach anyone beyond the three of us.

"Is this a *rape* whistle?" Mel asks, reaching for the discarded instrument on the table. "A little ill-suited for the occasion, no?"

Paige and I exchange a look.

"I didn't miss Luke, did I?" Calista asks, a trickle of water running freely down her chin. I wonder if she can even feel her face. How had she managed to get here by herself? I look around behind us, expecting to see the man whose boxers I saw that first visit to her place. Nothing but strangers.

"Luke's fourth. We have a little bit of time still," I say just as cheers erupt to welcome the first competitor to take the stage. He's wearing a tight-fitting tank top and black shorts that go down to his knees. From his expression alone, I can tell he's serious about his craft. But his song, "Beautiful Things" by Benson Boone, is going to clash with the current boisterous vibes of the bar. He points to an adorable woman in her early twenties at the table next to ours and says his performance is dedicated to Asha, his muse and the love of his life. Without her support, he never would have made it through his cancer treatments and he lives and breathes now solely for her. Politely, the crowd softens to hear the low, slow melody at the beginning of the song, and they put their drunken urges to catcall on hold while he performs.

Minutes later, he's hanging upside down with his arms outstretched as the song concludes; everyone is out of their seats to give a thunderous round of applause. Asha is a river of tears and so is the rest of her table, along with a smattering of random folks here and there. I can't help but wonder if I steered Luke in the wrong direction with the strip tease advice. Maybe this *is* more of a pole competition than a popularity or sexy time one, and I've set him up for disaster.

"Meh," Calista says, her head listing backwards then jerking forwards, her eyes widening at the realization she is still conscious and is at a bar. Mel's girlfriend nearly spits her drink out at the audacity of someone saying "meh" as a response to that heartfelt performance.

Oblivious to the stink eyes around her, Calista says, "He's not next, right? I have time to get a drink? Our parents can't make it; I really can't miss his act."

"Oh, god!" Sonya cries out. "I keep forgetting he's your little brother. Doesn't it bother you watching him–you know…" She puts her arms up as much as a person can in a crowded bar and shimmies her boobs.

Calista almost falls off her stool laughing. "He's not shaking tits. He doesn't even have any."

"You know what I mean," Sonya says, maintaining her upbeat persona, though now I can see the bit of annoyance in her eyes that I wouldn't have noticed before. "Pole dancing is one thing. A strip tease pole dance is something else altogether."

Calista makes a face as though she cannot fathom the stupidity of Sonya. "He's not a fucking stripper, Sonya, and that's not our target audience. We're rebranding away from that; Luke's aware."

It's like a movie that's put on pause. Everyone freezes: hands with drinks stopped midway to their mouths, jaws slackened and eyes all set on Calista. I doubt any of them have *ever* heard her speak like that based on what I've experienced day in and day out at the studio. The whistle, the high level of intoxication, and now yelling. No one knows what to think or how to respond.

It doesn't even sound like something Calista would say. Back during my time training with her, Calista commented multiple times how she contemplated doing some work at strip clubs to help raise money for her business before she got the inheritance.

Sonya's on the brink of crying. The rest of the studio will probably assume it's because of the random outburst, but I know on top of that she's freaking out at what Calista's response would be if she ever found out about Sonya's secret classes. If Calista would scream at her over a comment about sexy pole dancing, imagine how she'd react if she learned about her unauthorized lessons.

The awkward silence that follows is thankfully broken by the introduction of the next contestant. This one is tall, dark, and crazy handsome. He does a little rump shaking and a few decent pelvic rolls before mounting the pole. The moves were okay, clearly something added at the last minute and without too much prior preparation, but the crowd goes wild, regardless. This is what both sexes of the audience came for, a tame version of a strip club. Pole dancing is an art form, and an incredibly difficult one at that. But most people don't realize the extent of it; they immediately think of sexy time pole work. And so while a majority of this contest is blowing people's minds with complex tricks and the beauty of the moves, it's a good idea to feed their base desires with a smidge of seduction to go with it.

After the first two contestants, it's clear that Luke has this in the bag as long as Calista doesn't fuck it up for him with whatever crazy behavior she's about to let loose.

"Let's get you that drink," I shout to Calista over the cheers and screams from the crowd. Contestant number three is already up and dancing to "Save a Horse, Ride a Cowboy." Everyone treats this one like a group karaoke number.

"Yes!" she shouts back, her eyes wide with the anticipation of more booze that's not cheap beer.

Through a series of hand gestures and facial expressions, I communicate with Paige how I'm going to get Calista out of here just in case she loses her shit at Luke's dance, and I ask her to record it so I can watch it later. It breaks my heart a little that he's dancing for me and I won't be here in the audience to cheer him on, but I think he'd be on board with this plan. He's worked too hard for tonight to be ruined, and Calista needs someone sober to step in to save her from whatever self-sabotage she's currently engaging in.

For as drunk as she is, Calista's dancing background pays off as she snags her rape whistle, gracefully hops down from the stool, and is off, into the crowd behind us, before I can even grab my stuff. When I turn to chase after her, I bump face to tits into the woman behind me. She wraps her arms around me yelling, "Trixy! I thought that was you!"

CHAPTER 20
ANNA, SATURDAY, JULY 27TH

alista completely disappeared. I take my eyes off her bobbing and weaving head for half a second and poof, it's gone. Now I'm stuck in the arms of a woman who seems to be of medium build but has exceptional upper body strength. The crowd shouts, "and we made love!" signaling the impending end of the third contestant's song.

Shit.

"I had a feeling I was going to see you again," the woman yells into my ear over the crowd. When she pulls back and releases me, I see Molly staring back at me. The same Molly who had the tour guide go down on her in Italy and who was about to seduce the drunk Shakespeare guy the last time I saw her.

"Eddie!" she shouts to the man behind her. "This is Trixy. She was my waitress the night I met you."

My panic at the situation takes a back seat as I take in the stunning man in front of me. He literally looks like a model.

"A pleasure," he says to me with a genuine smile and a dip of the chin.

"Likewise," I manage.

"His name's Edmond, but he lets me call him Eddie. And

in the bedroom, he's sometimes Iago. Just like the night I met him."

"Nice," I say appreciatively, picturing this man as the sexy villain in Shakespeare's *Othello*.

Before Molly can get another word out, Iago's arms are around her waist and he bends down to ravish her neck with those soft lips and perfect amount of five o'clock shadow.

I have had nothing to drink, but my mind is swimming, regardless; it's a foggy mess from the overstimulation of everything. There's too much noise, too many people (Molly and Eddie included) on the verge of having public sex, too much at stake, and too many variables at play. The song is nearing its end and I have mere minutes now to find Calista, prevent her from drinking anything else, and get her the fuck out of here. But I also am genuinely intrigued that I've run into Molly again and don't want to leave her hanging.

Besides, it's not like I can quickly run off. It would be a slow departure of me unsuccessfully trying to part the crowd while leaving behind Molly and Eddie to either notice my gradual disappearance or to carry on with whatever they're about to do before realizing I'd rudely run off.

"Molly," I say to the woman whose face is tilted up to the ceiling and whose eyes seem to have rolled back a bit with the sudden rush of pleasure from Eddie's mouth on her neck.

"Trixy," she mimics back, her eyes still not focused on anything in particular.

"It was so fun running into you tonight and meeting Eddie, but I have to go." I'm already pushing through the crowds towards where I'm pretty sure the bar is located. "You should stop by for lunch sometime. That's the shift I work now," I call out over my shoulder before giving a final semi-rude nudge that forces me through a tight squeeze of people.

I'm relieved to see Calista leaning over the bar while all the bartenders actively ignore her. Either they know another drink is the last thing this wild woman needs, or they are truly overwhelmed with the bar reaching maximum capacity and Calista is conveniently falling through the cracks. It doesn't matter. Fate is finally throwing me a fucking bone, and I'm thankful.

"Calista!" I call out, waving my hands as I try to get her attention. Any second now, the MC is going to announce Luke and I need her out of the bar before that happens. She's too unhinged to be blindsided by his striptease.

"Calista!" I call again as I lose all decorum and start roughly shoving people aside. "I just heard Channing Tatum is outside." I have no idea if she's a fan or not, but what woman isn't?

Her eyes widen and her quest for alcohol takes a back seat as she grabs my wrist and drags me through the surge of people and towards the door.

We're so close I can hear random faint sirens coming from a block or two away. So damn close she gets her hands on the front door. That's when the MC shouts into the mic, "Make some noise for Luke from Art of Spinning."

Her inebriated squirrel brain forgets Channing Tatum (further proving how drunk she is) and we're now making our way back to the front stage. She's also let go of my wrist since I was only holding her back. I thought I was rude pushing my way through random strangers; Calista is a fucking terror.

"That's my brother!" she screams, followed by, "Art of Spinning changed my life! Best studio–" Then she's not shoving or screaming, and there's an hour-long minute where she's still and staring as Luke shimmies his jacket off his shoulders, his tie fluttering through the air, smacking into Calista's stunned face.

Before I can reach her, I see her right hand clutching the rape whistle, slowly bringing it up towards her mouth. My lead feet and legs won't move fast enough to stop her, and I know this. I understand the futility of trying to prevent that whistle from reaching her poised and ready lips. Instead of watching it happen, I look at Luke. I need to see him, in this moment, before Calista ruins it.

My god is this man beautiful. He exudes confidence in every sway of the hip, as if he's a professional adult dancer and this competition is another day for him. I think just about every woman and man in the room is momentarily picturing themselves up on stage with Luke, engaging in the same fantasy I'm having–where I'm merely existing and he's taking the lead to meet every single one of my desires via his dancing, and he's doing so effortlessly while looking like a million bucks.

The fantasy is interrupted when the fucking whistle starts up again. This time it's quick, successive blows to warn of danger or call attention. Luke is in a zone, unaffected by the noise, but the crowd is not immune and neither is the MC or any other staff member at the bar. Before I can reach her, the bouncer beats me to it and is gently guiding Calista out the main door while she argues about how she's not intoxicated, nor is she making a scene. Before "Slow Hands" even finishes, Calista is out on the street. I take one last look at Luke. He's at the trickiest part of his routine and I see him spinning, oblivious to the surrounding turmoil, as he nails his trickiest inversion.

CHAPTER 21
LUKE, SATURDAY, JULY 27TH

"Sonya," I half say, half ask when I see her approaching backstage. I was expecting an annoyed Calista or a flirtatious Jessi, not an anxious Sonya. This can't be good.

"We need to talk." She offers me a plastic cup full of a light beer, no doubt to soften whatever blow she's about to deal me. I decline. Based on the worry lines covering her forehead, it feels like I'm going to need a clear head tonight.

Minutes later, I'm breaking all etiquette for the competition and I'm in a cab on my way to Paige's apartment–the same apartment building where Jessi lives. On the short ride over, my mind mulls over what Sonya told me about Paige showing up and hugging Jessi, whispering to her the entire time she was there, and calling her Anna.

I also heard from Sonya about Calista's outburst. I couldn't hear or see much of anything with the speakers on the stage and the lights all pointed directly at me, so I didn't know anything about Calista's behavior. If it was anyone else telling me, I might question it. But Sonya has no reason to lie to me. There's zero benefit to her bringing up any of this since we already have a somewhat tenuous situation going with our mutual secrets.

According to her, the only reason she said anything to me about it is because she's worried about me. She wasn't before because I always had Calista, my big sister watching my back. That's not the case anymore, so she felt the need to temporarily step in with the sisterly advice since, according to her, I "have terrible taste in partners." She's convinced Jessi or Anna, or whatever her name is, isn't who she says she is.

It's too much for me to ignore, too. The past few weeks, I've been making excuses whenever my brain or gut lit up that something felt off. I've let our connection, her sweet smile, or my general admiration for her stomp down any uncertainties.

So stupid. The warning bells were ringing as soon as Calista announced the quick hire and that she'd be doing all the orientation stuff and paperwork herself.

I'm not convinced she's in the witness protection group like Florence said, but she has been lying to me about who she is, and I'm a mess of emotions now as the cab drives over the bridge.

There's anger, of course. But more so, there's a boulder of weight in my stomach at the thought that she didn't trust me. Whatever she's hiding, for whatever reason, she didn't trust me enough to let me in on it. It hurts.

My cab driver's eyes never leave the road. Where's the nosey PhD in psychiatry when you need him? I can hear his voice in my mind saying all the things that I should do: confront her immediately about it, stand up for myself and demand the truth, and for fuck's sake, clear things up with Calista.

I'm almost positive that's the sound advice the man would have given me, and yet I can't bring myself to do it. I see myself confronting Jessi in my mind, and then she comes back with a crazy explanation for all of it and I'm the asshole for thinking any differently. For not trusting her. Another part of me wants to keep waiting, to see how long she'd let this go before she admits she's been lying. Not that I'm completely sold on that idea; it's way too unrealistic. Could I really have sex with her again without knowing the truth?

Currently, she's at Paige's apartment with Calista. Another sure sign she does, in fact, know Paige. Why else would *she* be the one from the studio to help escort Calista home? She barely knows Calista. My sister's been missing in action for over a month, for as long as Jessi's been there. Yet another non-coincidence.

When I get up to the seventh floor of their apartment building, I find her and Paige sitting in the hallway, their backs against one of the apartment doors. It looks like it's been a night for both of them since they're each in comfortable shorts and tee-shirts. Nothing like what they were wearing before.

During the delay at the bar, I got to peek out from behind the curtain. I wasn't able to catch their attention, but I saw Paige and her, front and center at the high tops next to the stage. Her hair had light waves throughout and she was wearing a top that resembled a summery corset. I thought about how lucky I was that I was going to kick ass at this competition and then hopefully go back to her place and help her take off that lovely garment.

She's still a picture of perfection as she's leaning against the door with her hair now up and the corset long gone, but this is not how the night was supposed to go.

"Is Calista inside?" I ask once I'm halfway through the long hallway that goes down the length of the building.

"Yeah, she's fast asleep," Paige says as they both stand up.

"More like passed out," Jessi says, her eyes on Paige to see if she agrees or disagrees. Paige nods a confirmation.

"How did you do?" she asks me, her expression full of hope and optimism.

I give my head a quick shake. Another part of tonight that failed to live up to my expectations. A few of the ladies from the studio texted their condolences and said the typical responses of how I was robbed and how the winner, my nemesis, Marco, is a complete ass hat and unworthy of the title.

It's fine. The contest that I'd so badly wanted to win just a few hours before is now the last thing on my mind.

"I should go in and make sure Calista is still doing okay. My neighbor, she's an ER nurse, she says she should be fine. It's not alcohol poisoning. We put the puke bucket next to the couch, but I'm not convinced she'll find it if needed." Her hand on the knob, she adds, "It was good seeing you again, Luke. You were fantastic. Superb stuff." She gives me a sisterly squeeze on the arm. A kind gesture that goes straight to my heart given how my own sister is incapacitated and will probably not have kind words for me once she comes to.

Once Paige is back in her apartment, I eye up the exhausted, complicated woman in front of me. "Looks like we'll have to reschedule."

"Or," she says, her hand resting on the doorknob adjacent to Paige's, "we could DoorDash. We should talk."

I take in her apartment while she sits on the couch, probably thinking up how exactly she's going to explain that she's Paige's neighbor, even though minutes before we had sex, she lied to my face about not knowing Paige. I'm a generous man, so I give her time; it's going to take some real mental gymnastics to convince me. Or the better alternative: she's on the couch, mustering up the courage to spill it already and put everyone out of their misery by telling me the truth.

Since I'm hoping it's the latter, I don't push or rush her. Instead, I reluctantly look around the apartment, only to find myself falling harder for this woman.

It's smaller than mine, but nicer because she doesn't have to share with any roommates. There's a wall dedicated to the

Art of Spinning class calendar and I can't stop staring at it. Something similar would be perfect at the studio. A pain in the ass to keep up, for sure, but Calista's always talking about how the aesthetic of the studio is almost as important as the work that's done in it, and I full-heartedly agree. The competition is fierce in the city. If people are deciding to book a class based solely off of the images they found online, we'd better make sure ours are the best.

She also has the studio picture on the wall next to the calendar. The one that I took weeks before when the world made a lot more sense. I was so sure I'd win Pole Masters, help pull Calista out of whatever funk she was in, and permanently win over Jessi's heart in the process since she clearly has a thing for guys who can dance. In retrospect, it feels naïve.

"Paige and I have been neighbors for about ten years now," she says, her fingers twisting together in her lap. "Do you want to sit down? This could take a while."

It's a strained request, and I know it would help put her at ease if I took to the couch and sat with her, but I can't. For reasons I don't quite comprehend, I need to stand when I hear this. I shake my head and lean against a bookcase; she goes back to tangling her fingers and twisting her various rings.

"I'm from New York. Sunnyside, actually, though not this apartment building. One a few blocks down. I've never been to Pennsylvania, and I only applied to Juilliard. I didn't even land an audition."

I think back to the time she dodged my Juilliard question with a joke about how she took Strip Tease 101 there. The stone in my stomach increases in size and density. The lie had slipped out so easily, as if it hadn't affected her in the least. Obviously, I didn't believe that exact class existed in Juilliard's course catalogue, but that should have been the moment when she chose not to perpetuate the deception. It was the perfect time for her to say, "We should talk." Then I think about what we were doing when that conversation would have come up, and I'm not sure I can blame her for not wanting to kill the moment we were having.

She looks up at me now, her teeth worrying the corner of her lower lip. In her eyes there's a change, a dimming of the light. She thinks this is going to be the deal-breaker for me. Like I'm some sort of snob who was only interested in her because she went to Juilliard.

I should assure her that's not the case, but the words won't come. This isn't a small slight. As much as I never want to hurt her, I also can't jump at the chance to save her from this. She feels bad about lying. She should; it's warranted.

"Is your last name Brown?" I don't want to drag this out. She and Paige brought me here, to their side-by-side apartments, knowing the truth would have to come out, which is better than the alternative. I've seen desperate people dig themselves deeper, as if the solution to everything was just a few more shovels full of dirt away and they only needed to hunker down and keep digging.

She shakes her head. "Anna Laurier. Anna Leigh Laurier."

It's lovely. She's lovely. Anna Leigh Laurier. It repeats in my mind and I see it now. I remember in grade school having discussions with friends about names: if ours fit us, and if not, which name would be better. Mostly, we all agreed we couldn't imagine calling anyone by any other name. They just fit.

Maybe because I haven't known Anna as long as I'd known those friends, the name change happens effortlessly for me. Like a light going off in my mind, Jessi is gone. Anna is left, and she's just as I remembered her. Her lack of a Juilliard diploma doesn't make her any less of a capable dancer and artist.

But I still need to hear and understand whatever dubious morals she had that led her down this path of lies to begin with.

"I tried to tell you–"

"No," I say, cutting her off a bit more abruptly than I mean to. It sounds like she's about to start lying again and I don't know if I can take it.

"I signed an NDA." Her words cut through my thoughts. Maybe Florence was closer than she realized with that witness protection nonsense.

"With the government?"

She opens her mouth, closes it, and then tries again. "With Calista. It came from her lawyer."

I shake my head and silently curse Calista with everything I have. What the fuck was she thinking?

"That's not a real NDA." I don't go into the details about how Calista cut costs over a year ago by moving from someone who passed the bar and has an actual brain, to AI. She's been using it for all of her official business paperwork: job descriptions, termination paperwork, and even our mission statement at the studio. There is very little chance the nondisclosure agreement would stand up in court, and even less chance Calista would go through the hassle of hiring a real lawyer to sue Anna.

I'm feeling every emotion imaginable, and yet I'm still able to give a soft laugh at Anna's grumpy reaction to what I've said. She's adorable even when she's annoyed.

I can also feel my anger continuing to fade with this new revelation. I'm still not sure what the endgame was with this whole alter ego, but it puts my mind at ease knowing she felt legally compelled to keep it up. In her mind, she took a risk telling me about it tonight.

"But…"

"It's AI generated. Did you read through it? I bet it's full of errors."

Her hands fall to her sides and she presses her palms against the cushion, as if bracing herself or helping to keep an upright posture when all she wants to do is collapse into nothingness.

"I didn't read… It all happened so fast!"

I join her on the couch. It won't do any good to punish or push blame at this point. Calista may have been the one pulling all the strings, but Anna and I have both made mistakes in how we've handled this.

"I know," I say, knowing very little about what actually happened, but feeling like I have to say something, anyway. In a way, it's the truth. I know what it feels like to float along with a current, all the way through to the waterfall at the end. It's only when you look back and see all the rocks, whirlpools, and venomous snakes in the water that you realize you'd been in danger the whole time and had chosen to ignore it by blissfully gazing up at the cloudless sky instead.

"She and Paige ambushed me at the restaurant–I work a second job at Pizzano's Pizza Palace–and they invited me back to Calista's place after my shift. She convinced me to take over her classes, and while I was working, I was supposed to get close to the staff so I could figure out who was stealing money from the studio. Not literally stealing money, but she said someone was doing something shady that was killing her finances, and I assumed it was theft or something similar."

"What?" I actually see red for a second when I hear this.

I'm back up from the couch, pacing the entirely too short hallway in Anna's apartment. Calista's done some mildly questionable things in the past–mostly in her teens and early twenties–but this is too much.

"She gave me the fake name so the staff couldn't find me on social media and put together that I was friends with Paige. She didn't want anyone to connect me to her. No one could know that I knew Calista outside of work. She said they wouldn't trust me if they had even the slightest suspicions about us knowing each other beyond the studio."

I can't help it. Exhaustion and irritation seep into my voice. "And you went along with this?"

"She offered me $5k up front and more when I figured it all out. It sounded lucrative and noble. I'd be helping her save her company from a crook and making a little much needed money while I was doing it."

More pieces fall into place. Her curiosity with the whole Sonya situation, for one. Everything else is minor: questions, looks, and comments that may or may not have been innocent. Her entire existence at the studio now, every interaction we've had, I'm not sure what to make of it. Was she interested in me, or just interested in seeing if I had any dirt on my coworkers? The thought spirals into a more disturbing realization.

"And she suspected me, too?"

Anna looks up to the ceiling for an answer, then says, "I don't know. She didn't tell me anything. Really. Calista said the best way to tackle it was to send me in blind rather than potentially lead me in the wrong direction with whatever ideas she had about what was happening."

We sit with this for a beat before she continues. "I didn't know you were related until after the first class. Paige told me."

My mind races, trying to determine if I've ever experienced a betrayal as severe as this one. I'm desperate for personal reference on how to proceed, but since this is an unprecedented level of deception, my brain has nothing for me. I also can't pinpoint which hurts worse, the secrecy from my sister with this crazy, paranoid story about potential fraud at the studio, or Anna secretly spying on me and lying the entire time we've been together.

"Say something, please. Tell me what you're thinking. Ask me anything." Her eyes are brimming with tears that won't fall.

"What did you tell Calista?"

"Nothing. There's nothing to tell."

"What about Sonya's night classes?"

"No!" she blurts out, forceful enough to kill any doubt I might have. "What she's doing is not great," she says slowly, giving careful consideration to each word. "But I don't think that's what Calista was after. Giving off-the-books after-hours lessons is a legal hazard and a form of theft, but it wouldn't be affecting her books that much. I don't think Sonya's secret classes are what Calista was after."

I let out a deep breath. Sonya has a lot of shit in her life right now; losing that extra income and potentially losing her job could break her mentally and send her and her family out onto the streets.

"And I haven't said anything about Florence, but I would monitor her."

"Florence?" I repeat, assuming I must have misheard her. "What is Florence doing?"

"She has a business model on her computer for a new company that would take over Art of Spinning. Same building and some of the same employees, but a burlesque kind of place instead of a pole studio."

Ironically, Anna sounds like Florence with this nonsensical conspiracy theory.

"I can't get into this anymore. Not tonight," I say, heading for the door. I've only just begun the messy work of reconciling everything I thought I knew a few hours earlier, with all the new information I'm hearing now. I need some space before I say something I'm going to regret.

CHAPTER 22
ANNA, SATURDAY, JULY 27TH

close my eyes and press my lips together, unable to fathom how this has unfolded exactly how Paige said it would. Can I really say I'm blindsided when she warned me hours earlier how this conversation would go down? She'd been the one encouraging our hook up all along, but only because she thought it was innocent flirting and maybe a one-night-stand. Once she saw our text exchange out in the hallway, and after I'd filled her in on some of our conversations, gave her the CliffsNotes version of our time in the office and in Shakespeare's Garden, Paige changed her opinion on the matter.

"I'm sorry," I say, my voice louder than necessary given our proximity. But it works. He pauses and turns to look at me, and all I see is my future. Behind him, to the left, is my chalkboard wall full of all the activities I love, and to the right is the picture he took where I look like I am the happiest woman that has ever lived because in that moment, through the intense pain of a still semi-noob holding that difficult pose, I truly was that happy. And then there's Luke in the middle of it all. This is supposed to be my future, and if I don't fight for it now, I will surely lose it all.

I feel like the lion who was born and raised in a cage, and then finally released out into the wild. The freedom and sense of lightness I've felt these past two months is unmatched to anything I've experienced in my adult life. Losing Luke and the studio is the equivalent of shoving me back into the cage.

I refuse to go back. I cannot.

"I'm sorry about the lies, and I'm sorry about getting in the middle of what's clearly a messy situation between you and your sister. But that's it. I'm not sorry for anything that you and I did, and that was all me, by the way. Going by the name Jessi, sure, but I was the one doing and saying it all. You were falling for me; it was always me."

I'd questioned it myself, in the beginning. There was this unshakable feeling that I was falling back into my acting ways and taking on the role of Jessica Brown. But honestly, after that first night when we had drinks after class, I'd stopped feeling like I was playing a part. The personality was all mine, only I'd needed help to find it again. And I did, thanks to the studio and the lovely people working there with me.

"I need to think, *Anna*," he says with slight derision in his voice that about sends me into a rage.

"No. Don't," I say back sternly.

"You're mad at me?" he scoffs, his feet planted in front of the door.

"If you're going to march out of here like a victim and not at least hear me out? Yes, that sucks and I'm going to be mad about it."

"You *lied* to me. You lied to everyone. This is the natural consequence of that. I'm going to be mad for more than five minutes. Deal with it."

"You don't know what I'm dealing with right now. My life has been absolute shit with a crappy job I hate, bills I can't get ahead of, and a meal plan that consists of eating as much free pizza as I can get from Papa Pizzanos. But something tells me you and your sister have never been that poor. Have never had to prioritize your water bill over your electricity bill after one hospital stay completely wiped out your savings. Am I right?"

His eyes don't leave mine, and he doesn't hang his head in shame. I can tell he's waging a war of arguments in his mind trying to decide if he had been in a similar situation, if he could have been provoked into performing unethical tasks for life-changing money and the promise that the work was, in the end, on the right side of things even if felt wrong the entire time he was doing it.

"I am sorry for not telling you the whole truth." I put my hand up to stop him from stating the obvious, which is that I flat out lied and did not just withhold some truthful aspects of the story. "When I was first offered the job, I financially could not refuse. My life is 100 times better with that extra money. And because of the NDA, the possibility of that money being taken back from me along with whatever legal fees I would have to deal with… It wasn't an option for me to break that. I wanted to every second of every day once I got to know you, but I could not."

He nods like he understands, but his expression says he doesn't.

"What was the endgame? If tonight hadn't happened, when were you going to tell me? *Were* you going to?"

I'm up now, too. Against my better judgment, my finger is up and pointed at him.

"Yes, I was always going to tell you everything tonight. I planned to confront Calista tonight about how crazy this entire scheme was, and how I didn't find anything because she has a lovely crew of people working for her. I was going to mention that maybe Florence was planning some sort of hostile takeover, but really, even that felt unlikely and not worth mentioning. And then, after the competition, when we were going to share a cab back to my place, I was going to tell you on the drive over. I would have explained why Paige was in the backseat with us, going back to the same building we were."

My tone fizzled quickly with that last bit. He's right. I was so stuck on how and when I'd talk to Calista that I hadn't really planned that far in advance for how I'd tell Luke afterwards. Hadn't really accepted that it would actually happen. For the longest time, it was a distant date and time, and I could ignore it while focusing on what was going on in the immediate present.

"Does your cousin really have a three-legged dog?" His voice lacks bite and his facial expressions softened.

"Yes!" Again, way too loud for two feet that separate us. But he's warming up to me, and the threat of going back into the cage is falling away. "And we really do call him Legster."

"Did your mom split a pork roll with Ron Jeremy the last time she was up visiting you?"

I grimace and he runs his fingers through his hair before taking off his glasses and pinching the bridge of his nose. I push out all thoughts of how fucking sexy he is when he's all serious and flustered like this, especially because it's aimed in my direction.

"I said that one of my first days at work," I say, careful to keep my voice steady and not too aggressive. "It was literally part of my job to make friends with everyone. Mel was talking about pork rolls and I'd heard Florence going on and on about all the 'Big Brother' seasons... It was like killing two birds with one stone. And only a half lie, really, since Mom did once have a pork roll experience with someone who looks a lot like Ron Jeremy. Practically a doppelgänger."

"How can I even trust you?" he asks. He means it, too. This isn't a rhetorical question that's huffed out before someone stomps away. He's practically begging me to explain to him how he can put this behind him and trust me again.

"You stay."

It feels like I'm not just pleading with him; I'm putting this one out to the universe. Luke, the studio, the class calendar on the wall. I'm begging for it not to be taken away from me. Deep down I had a feeling, a premonition that this could and would crash and burn. I might as well have signed that NDA with my blood; it was always a deal with the devil.

I only signed because I couldn't fathom how much of an impact this studio would have on me. I didn't expect to fall in love with Luke and all the ladies. Working somewhere else isn't the magical solution to this. Art of Spinning, as it is right now, is a unique entity. So even if it really is over between Luke and me, he and I still need to figure out what's next with Calista. Shit's getting real and ignoring it only puts everyone at risk. Even wildly successful companies can be taken down in a blaze of glory if the CEO isn't in the right mind to run things.

"If nothing else," I say, the pressure of defeat weighing heavy on me but not completely taking me out of the equation, "let me help you. With Calista."

Luke puts his glasses back on, gives a slow, sad shake of his head, and lets himself out of my apartment.

CHAPTER 23
LUKE, SUNDAY, JULY 28TH

spent the night in the studio. There's a decent sized couch in our lobby area, and not a soul in sight–exactly what I needed.

Gabe and I have become good friends, someone I see myself still hanging out with even after we've moved out of the apartment and have gone our separate ways, but he's out in terms of guy advice. Having a girlfriend has sent him too far into romantic optimism territory. He wouldn't be an unbiased shoulder to lean on; he'd be a secret spy for love, pretending to be indifferent while only pushing me back into Anna's embrace.

Even without that pro-love encouragement, I spent half the night tossing and turning, wondering why I'd stomped off, leaving Anna and her perfectly good bed for the lumpy couch that's had hundreds of asses on it throughout its lifetime.

The studio's first class is at seven in the morning, and I'd stupidly set my alarm to make sure I was up well before that. As if I really thought I'd get the best sleep of my life and wouldn't be able to get my ass off of this couch.

I'm behind the desk on the computer when I hear Florence come in.

Her face registers immediate disgust. "Ugh, you didn't sleep here, did you?"

I comb my fingers through my already styled hair. It's not the first time I've crashed here, so I've already done a quick washcloth bath, brushed my teeth and hair, and changed my clothes.

She sighs. "You did. You need to grow up, Luke," she chastises before doing a quick lean over the counter. "Is Jessi here?"

"Jessi Brown?" I say with too much bitterness. All last night, I found my anger being tampered by the details of her arrangement with Calista. I want to be pissed, but it's not coming as easily as I thought it would. Even now I'm debating if I want to blow up Anna's spot or not with Florence.

"You're acting weird. Are you still drunk?" She takes in a whiff of the air around me but isn't satisfied.

"I'm not drunk; I didn't drink last night."

"There's no shame in having your ass handed to you by Marco, and there's no shame in drowning your sorrows in a bottle or two of Jack."

"Have you *ever* seen me have more than a drink?"

"Here? No. But I don't know what you do outside these walls."

As I try to wrap my head around Florence's insistence that I have a drinking problem, I notice movement through the glass of the front door and find, to my absolute horror, I'm at the door. I'm wearing the same tiny shorts I wore last night–slightly skimpier than what I normally wear because I really, really wanted to win and my desperation came out in my outfit choice–and I'm in the middle of a sexy serenade. I'm also made of cardboard and being man-handled by Lyric as she struggles to get the life-sized cardboard cut-out into the studio.

A true gentleman would have dropped everything to help, but I'm literally incapable as my brain is taking every ounce of energy I have to process what it is I'm seeing.

"Luke!" Lyric chastises once she's fully in the studio and finds me behind the desk next to Florence. "You're not even scheduled today. Why are you always here?"

"He got trashed last night and crashed on the sofa, or maybe the floor somewhere. He was already awake when I came in," Florence explains.

Lyric's annoyance dissolves, and in its place is pity. "Tough loss last night. Joined in on Calista's bender, huh?"

"No! I wasn't drinking last night. You all were."

"Socially, Luke," says Florence. "There's a difference."

I'm not going to convince them otherwise, and at this point, my frustration is to where I can't find the will to care. They think I got smashed and slept it off on the lobby floor? So be it.

"Why is there a giant cut-out of me, almost naked, in the lobby?" The more I look at it now, the more it looks like my black shorts are a sensor, and I'm actually naked with a black bar over my crotch.

"Well…" says Lyric, a smile coming back to her face, "it was supposed to be a surprise."

"What's supposed to be a surprise?"

"This!" Her face is a mixture of pride and confusion. "I convinced Calista to let me get it for my bachelorette parties. Our props were getting old and out-dated. It was also supposed to be in the lobby, when we're not doing parties, with some sort of sign or lettering nearby saying you were the Pole Masters champion of July 2024."

I can't take my eyes off myself. It's all too weird. Calista has used the excuse of opening another location for why she's been missing in action lately, but now it's been months with nothing to show for it. No address for this mysterious new location or any word on staffing for it or potential dates for when it will open. She got hammered before the competition, yelled at Sonya (according to Sonya) and convinced Anna to lie to everyone to find a crook who doesn't even exist. And now, finally, she authorized this almost nude cut-out of me for drunk bachelorettes to pose with for pictures.

While I process it all, Florence types away at the computer—scheming to take over while Calista is out of the picture?—and Lyric digs a few nipple tassels from her bag and puts them on, pleased that she can show me one of the ways my cut-out can be altered for maximum bachelorette fun.

"I need to find Calista," I say, grabbing my phone and keys and darting around my naked self to get to the front door.

Just as I'm walking out into what is already sweltering hot, humid weather, I think I hear Florence say, "Did you see this email from Jessi?" I roll my eyes. I wonder what lies she has for them today.

I text Paige and she says Calista left really early in the morning, before she even got up. I assume she's at home. Maybe licking her wounds or getting ready to ream me out for not adequately representing the studio. Maybe something else entirely that I can't even imagine, because for the first time in my life, I feel like I barely know my sister.

It's walking distance from the studio and not yet Satan's-oven hot temperature wise, so I forgo the cab and take the journey on foot. I figure I can text her on the way over and possibly clear my head a bit.

"Morning," I say to the doorman with a nod of my head when I finally arrive. "Here to see Calista Plato." I'm only at Calista's place maybe once a year, so I can't remember his name, but he's been the doorman for a few years now, so he should recognize me. And yet, like so many other things that have happened in the few scant hours I've been conscious this morning, today is the exception.

The man, Herman, I see glancing down at the name badge, steps in front of the doors. He doesn't raise his arms or touch me, but I wouldn't put it past him if I kept going.

"Is there a problem?" I ask, looking over his shoulder, as if Calista would not let me in, but then would also stand in the lobby watching me not get into the building.

Herman looks confused. "Have you spoken with her lately?" He's still blocking the doors to the entrance, his feet spaced shoulder width apart and his hands together in front of him, but his broad shoulders say this relaxed stance could change in an instant if need be.

"Just last night," I lie. The hypocrisy isn't lost on me, but there's no time to dwell on it.

"And she knows you're coming here? To see her?" He's looking at me like I'm the insane one. Like I haven't been coming over to see Calista for the past almost decade, even if my visits were at best sporadic.

"Yes," I say heatedly before I immediately deflate, thanks to an old memory. I once opened the door to a police officer late at night. My mom yelled at me for opening the door, but I didn't see the issue. The guy was in a uniform and he was smiling when I looked through the peephole. Seconds later, when he was talking to my mom and verifying if my dad lived there and was her husband. I saw through his facial expressions and I knew Dad wasn't okay. Before he even said the word accident and hospital, I just knew.

This is the feeling I have now. I know Calista is not in that building, and somehow I know I will never enter it again to see her, even though I'm only going off the facial expressions of a stoic, mostly silent doorman.

"She's not in there, is she?"

He shakes his head. I wonder if he's even allowed to tell me this, or if the head shake is a loophole in the system where he's technically not telling me private information about occupants.

"You're expecting her back later?"

Another head shake and the slight squinting of his kind eyes. He wants to tell me what's going on, but his job won't allow it. I've heard that one before. I get it.

"Thanks, Herman," I say, with a final nod and one last look at the building before I head back to the studio.

CHAPTER 24
ANNA, SUNDAY, JULY 27TH

"I should probably tell you a few things about Calista," Paige says, pushing around the eggs and buttered toast on her plate.

She texted early saying Calista was once again missing in action and asking if Luke was still here. When I told her no, she insisted on coming over.

"This sounds like you're about to tell me a lot of stuff I probably should have known before I signed a contract with her."

The bitterness spreads too easily for me. I know I made my own decisions with Calista. I chose to ignore all the red flags that I'd seen, but maybe if we'd all discussed things as they happened, and I mean all as in everyone at the studio, we wouldn't be in this situation where it's suddenly escalated to where we don't know how to fix it.

She gives the slightest head tilt, a hint of acquiescence to what I've said. Paige is a parent dealing with a hostile toddler and trying to be patient while the toddler unleashes unchecked emotions on everyone around them. A bit of grace for the sake of friendship. I know all of this, but I don't apologize. Later, I'm sure, but I can't manage it here at the table when I know things are going to get much worse before they get better.

"Calista and I were roommates throughout college. That first year it was by chance; we were strangers."

"I know all of this," I say, lazily rolling my wrist in the universal gesture for let's get on with it. The blade has been dangling over my neck for far too long. I need it to drop and put me out of my misery.

"I thought I knew Calista after living with her that first year, but I didn't. Not really. A year sounds like forever when you're occupying a tiny room together, but we were both private people. Our friendship was surface level. We picked each other as roommates for the next year because we knew we could stand to live together. It was that year, our sophomore year, that Calista fell into a bit of a depression. Or maybe it was something else; I'm still not sure."

Now she has my attention. It's hard to imagine vibrant, attack-the-world Calista struggling with something like depression. I think back to that first night when she'd danced to "Cough Syrup" by Young the Giant. The beautiful, haunting lyrics and the way she danced with her whole heart, as if she were the one to write the words and melody, and she was bringing the whole thing together in dance to put the final nail in the coffin of her demons. But maybe it didn't work.

"How bad?" The two words represent a million other questions that don't feel fit to be said aloud.

"Honestly, I didn't even realize until the second semester. We moved back in after winter break and I noticed she'd lost some weight. Her clothes were hanging off of her. Not long into the semester, I came down with strep throat and felt like death for a week. That's when I saw Lizzy was in the dorm with me most of that week. She wasn't going to half her classes; she'd dropped out of her clubs. It felt like she was sleeping just as much as I was. Before that, I'd figured if I caught her sleeping, she was just getting in a quick nap before running off to whatever list of things she had to complete that day."

While we nibble at our food, Paige details out a few specific incidents and how she got Calista's parents involved, but they weren't much help. In the end, their response was that Calista did that sometimes, and it was best to wait her out. She'd snap out of it eventually; stop being so dramatic.

"They were right. Kind of. A month before the end of the semester, she wasn't home when I got back from class. For the rest of the year, I barely saw her. She re-joined all the clubs with excuses and apologies. I only overheard one of those phone calls; she told them about her sick family member and a few other things. I can't remember specifics now. I just know that what she told them was not what happened.

"I never said anything though because it was okay again. I even forgot about the whole thing until our senior year. By then, we were a lot closer. Like sisters. Sometimes things would get rough for a week or two, and then she'd bounce back again. Or maybe it was longer than that. This all feels like another lifetime. It's been so long since it happened. But just a few weeks into our last year, she disappeared into herself again. I mean, she really went down hard and for more than a few weeks. This time, I felt ready. I didn't involve her parents; I convinced her to go to the on-campus doctor. We never talked about it outright after I'd taken her to her appointment, but she slowly started getting better again."

I thought about what she said. If somehow I'd known that Calista had mental health struggles way back in college, would that have affected my decision? Would it have stopped me from eagerly signing that NDA and embarking on this crazy journey? I doubt it. I wouldn't have wanted that anyway. As much as I feel like I'm in a shit position now, I still prefer this to the life I had before.

"You know I couldn't tell you any of that, right?" She puts

down her fork, officially done pushing around what she'll never eat. "Calista deserves better than that. She's more than what she's battling right now. I'm only letting you in on her past because it sounds like maybe that's what's happening now, and I want to help if I can."

"But last night, she was as alive as I've ever seen her. This doesn't sound–"

"It's exactly the same. There were a few random times here and there in the middle of an *episode,* I'll say, for lack of a better term. A few bursts of energy that usually involved booze or even blow one night, and then she was down again like it never even happened. I thought she was sleeping off the hangover, but days and weeks would go by again before she'd really get up and out of bed and do something beyond the very basics of maintaining life."

We go back and forth about it. The timing doesn't add up for me. The initial proposition, the weeks we'd spent together training. It seems impossible that the person I was interacting with all that time was successfully battling depression or some sort of mental health crisis. Then I realize I probably sound like her parents and feel ashamed. I need to accept that I do not know Calista nearly as well as everyone else does. If Luke and Paige say there's a problem, I need to trust them.

Once we've covered Luke's concerns about everything as well, she asks about last night. I could have kept the charade going, acted like I lived on a different floor and what a crazy coincidence it was that Paige, Calista's college roommate, lives in the same building as me and we'd never, ever met. But to what end? At some point, I needed to stop digging the hole and start working on a way out of the abyss I was creating.

I told her about our conversation and how I'd come clean and so close to convincing him everything that happened between us was real. It was literally just a different name and a tiny adjustment to my background. The looks, the chemistry, the teasing, the conversations, the flirtation. All of that was real. It was me, regardless of what name he was calling me.

"And then he left." I go back to eating my now cold breakfast. Comfort eating is my go-to when I'm stressed. Paige slides her plate towards me. She knows the drill.

"He'll come around." Her voice is gentle but firm. A reassuring confidence that lets me push it to the back of my mind so we can focus on the more timely and pressing details: what to do about Calista and how to tell the rest of the staff about who I really am.

"Work email," Paige says, like it's the most obvious solution and other alternatives aren't worthy of discussion.

"No way. It's too impersonal. I've lied to everyone's face for over a month. I can't just email them about it."

"Yes, you absolutely can and will."

"How many years have you been working from home now?"

"A lot, but I'm still right. This is going to be an elaborate reveal with lots of parts to it. A well-crafted email that you can edit over and over again until it's perfect is the only way to go here. If you try to do this in person, you're going to fuck it up and there's too much at stake for that."

"Yeah, no. This is a bad idea." I look down at my empty plate and debate making another egg. Maybe I can swing by that coffee place on my way to the studio, grab a doughnut to keep the nerves down before I start in on my many apologies to everyone.

"Please listen to me. Even if you successfully tell someone, they will fuck it up in the retelling as they text or Snap your other coworkers to give them the latest tea." When I don't respond, she adds, "You have to get ahead of this and you have to do it now. It's not like you wanted to deceive everyone. You went in thinking this was a virtuous assignment with slightly unethical means. That's what you need to explain; that's what other people retelling the story are going to forget or leave out."

This is accurate. One of the pole instructors at Art of Spinning quit a few weeks before I started there. The rumors about why she quit and how she did it were impressive. Half the staff was convinced the woman had a fatally ill secret lover on the west coast that she needed to care for. Turns out it was her mother, not a lover, and her husband and kids were all moving out west with her since the mother was ill but not fatally ill.

I give a dramatic sigh that makes Paige practically giddy. "You're writing this for me, right?"

"I'll pretty it up, but it has to be yours. Otherwise, you're still lying when I type the email and it comes from your address and your signature down at the bottom."

"Fine. You'll write it with me."

"How long do we have? When's your lunch shift start?"

My stomach roils at the thought of serving today. I'm not in the mood, and working as a server in this mind frame is difficult. Without a permanent smile on my face, some asshole is liable to tell me to smile more or that I look prettier when I smile, and then I'll be tempted to smash his skull in with a pepper flake shaker.

"I have a few hours."

"Plenty of time." Paige cracks her knuckles and grabs my computer once I'm logged in. "Okay," she says, fingers poised over the keys, ready to dance out an apology that will have the other employees begging forgiveness, even though I'm the one in the wrong. "You talk; I'll type it up all pretty."

"Trixy!" Molly calls as she and Iago (I can't remember his real name) are following the hostess to a two top in my section.

I cannot get over how this woman declared almost two months prior, at the table next to the one she's at now, that she was going to seduce the Drunk Shakespeare guy, and she's now brought back said Drunk Shakespeare guy having accomplished her goal. Who does that?

I try not to stare at Iago, though I may be the only one. The hostess, other patrons, and half the staff are all shamelessly gawking at the immaculate hottie sitting in my section. Molly's either unaware or used to it by now, and Iago has no idea because he only has eyes for her. I feel a stabbing pain in my heart, thinking about how Luke once looked at me that same way.

"Molly, Iago," I say when I arrive at their table for drink orders.

"Eddie, please," he says with a sweet smile. "We looked for you again last night, but you vanished."

After looking around at all the tables to double-check they'd survive without me for five minutes, I give the most succinct run-down I can of what happened.

Eddie looks perplexed, but only mildly. Shakespeare is known for his crazy alternate identity plot lines. This is probably tame to what he acts out on a regular basis.

Molly's rapt. I didn't mention that I've never been to Italy, but I think it's safe to say she may have picked up on it. That doesn't seem to bother her, though; I think the story in itself is enough to overlook everything else. I remember from that night how she and her friends loved a good story; loved them enough to keep traveling the world to create them.

"Did anyone email you back? What did they say?" she asks, desperate for all the dirt.

"I don't know. I left my phone in my work locker. Just keep delaying the inevitable, you know?"

Eddie excuses himself to use the facilities, and Molly insists I plop down next to her at the table. Why not? I'm at that point where things are so low, I can't seem to care if I'm making them worse. I might get fired? Good. I need a powerful fire under my ass to start getting my shit together and making better choices. I need to be doing things that make me happy rather than miserable.

I even munch on one of the breadsticks in their complementary bowl. I feel better already.

"I have nothing for you. That is a hell of a story. You don't mind if I tell the girls, do you? We're heading to Belize in a few months."

I shrug. The bread is soothing; I can't find the will to care.

"Oh, you know what?" She grabs her purse and starts rummaging through all sorts of random stuff. "Hmm, it's not here. I must have lost it or maybe I threw it out when I cleaned out my purse last week."

I keep munching. Unless she's searching for a check for a couple grand or a version of Luke who doesn't hate me, there's nothing in there that can save me from the comfort of hiding out in my little hole of despair.

"Yup, business card is gone," says Molly, ignoring how rude I'm being by eating their last breadstick. "No worries. We don't need a card. I have a friend of a friend who runs a pole dancing studio in Cobble Hill." She grabs a napkin and a pen from her purse so she can write down the information. "I hope this thing at Art of Spinning works out for you, but if it doesn't, you should look into this one. My work friends and I went pole dancing there when we did a summer bingo thing one year. We were all crap at it, but we had the best time. Seriously, they were amazing."

I take the napkin and stare at the information, willing it to give me some sort of feeling or insight about if this is a viable alternative for me.

"Tell them I sent you, if you go. And you can use me as a reference if you apply for a position there."

Eddie's back and the host is seating a five top in my section, so I'm up again and back to a job that I hate. It's not horrible right now, but I doubt Eddie and Molly will frequent the restaurant nearly enough to take the sting off everything else I hate about this job.

Still, I put on my best smile and head for the five-top with the expensive-looking Lego shopping bags. If they've dropped a few hundred on toys, hopefully they can spare a few twenties for me, too.

If I want to try out another studio, I'll probably have to do it as a customer before I'm able to get another teaching gig. And if I want to afford a pole class in Cobble Hill, I'm going to need these tips now more than ever.

CHAPTER 25

LUKE, SUNDAY, JULY 27TH

There are seven people in the lobby when I get back to the studio, even though only one person, Sonya, is scheduled to instruct a class.

"You slept with Jessi?" Nautica asks when I walk in, her two-month-old coincidentally giving me a matching confused look as he sits in the carrier strapped to her chest.

"I... What?" I stammer.

"Not Jessi. Anna," Lyric says, correcting Nautica.

"You're surprised?" Florence asks in a way that drips with sarcasm. "Have you seen them together?"

"She hasn't; her water broke a month before Anna got here."

Once again, they turn to study me, their eyes unwittingly darting back and forth between my clothed human form and my unclothed cardboard form standing next to me.

"You didn't read the email?" Nautica asks, not caring that I haven't answered her first question.

"I've been busy."

I don't want to talk about Anna. Calista is at the forefront of my mind. I can't believe my good fortune that so many staff members are randomly at the studio so early this morn-ing, but they're not here to tackle the Calista dilemma; they're here to gossip in person about whatever Anna wrote in that email. Isn't this what SnapChat is for? So people can talk with a group of friends from anywhere in the world rather than gather in person?

"You *have* to read it. So good. I mean, a bit messed up, but I get it," says Lyric.

The AC kicks in and I feel the cool breeze against my neck, and the tickle of the fluttering nipple tassels that still adorn my cardboard self. I ignore all of that as I scan the faces of the women looking back at me: curiosity, intrigue, pity, and other similar emotions. And yet I don't see anger or resentment. It must have been one hell of an email; too bad I'm nowhere near ready to read it, assuming it's a version of what she told me last night.

"And you're all okay with that? With her lies?" I ask.

Is everyone in the world a better person than I am? Am I the asshole for being mad at the long-term deception? Because from what I can tell, everyone is ready to switch over from Jessi to Anna without giving it another thought. They'll go about their days as if it was all some silly minor mistake, and now that it's cleared up, there's no reason to harp on it.

"For fuck's sake," Florence says, thoroughly done with me barging in on their conversation without having completed the required reading. "Go up into the office and read the damn email."

"She told me last night–"

"Luke!" half of them yell back at me, with Nautica providing earmuffs for the little one who's growing tired and ready to take a nap against his mother's chest.

"Okay! Okay." I put my hands up in defense. When no one comes at me physically (not that I thought they would) I pull my phone from my back pocket, but decide against reading it while they all stare at me, waiting for my reaction.

"I'll be up in the office."

I don't immediately open my email. Instead, I sit and think about the other significant Anna moment I had in this same office. It wasn't like the parties I'd had before, those random women. Anna's anything but some meaningless hookup. Sure, I saw stars and literally collapsed on her shoulder afterwards, but it's more than that. Vulnerability, intimacy, respect, communication. Does it matter that I didn't know her name, or that some of what I thought I knew about her, like her graduation from Juilliard or her mother sharing a sandwich with Ron Jeremy, didn't happen? I sit for at least thirty minutes, rolling it all back and forth in my mind while I twist and turn the chair as much as the limited office space will allow.

After an impressive amount of stalling that included a little paint touch-up on the Leslie Knope potted plant, I relent and open the email.

Subject: Please Read to the End

Art of Spinning Family,

On Wednesday, June 5th, my life changed forever. I signed on to become an instructor at Art of Spinning, and agreed to do so under the fake name of Jessica Brown.

My real name is Anna Laurier. I'm a NYC native. I only completed a few semesters at Hunter College; that is my only college experience.

I won't bore you with the backstory of how it came about, but I can tell you that when I agreed to come on board and deceive my future coworkers, I had no idea it would snowball the way that it did.

I convinced myself it wouldn't matter that coworkers didn't know my real name or have all the details about my past. Every job I've had, I barely knew the people I worked with and they often were in and out of my life like a revolving door since I tended to work in retail and restaurants.

I couldn't have predicted Art of Spinning would become a home to me, and that you all would become family.

Mel, you tell the best stories, where the people listening feel like they were there, too.

Lyric, if I were ever to get married, I'd come to you for my bachelorette party. Your energy and excitement for each bride is inspiring. How do you celebrate them all as if they're your favorite sister?

The list continues. She mentions every staff member, including Calista, and details out what she loves most about working with them. Once she's buttered up the staff, convincing us that she truly likes us, she lists out some fabrications she's mentioned over the past month. Despite everything, I chuckle at the absurdity of it all. She admits her mom didn't have lunch with Ron Jeremy, that she's never had a driver's license and therefore never cried to get out of a speeding ticket, and that she didn't go streaking with a group at Juilliard across the bridge connecting the residence halls to the main campus.

She also had a section where she felt compelled to admit to things that didn't involve any lying, but would be considered somewhat unethical, if not illegal. The woman purged all her guilt this morning.

Aside from the lies, I also need to apologize for the time I took extra doughnuts from the box. I had my period, and the cravings made me do it.

I'm also sorry I snuck the extra doughnuts into the studio and took secret bites in the back of the room while I pretended to check something in my bag. Again, my period made me do it.

And finally, I'm not sorry that Luke and I had sex, but I am sorry we did it in the office during studio hours.

I shake my head at the last paragraph, but I can't help smiling, either. I kept my feelings for Anna to myself mostly because I'm a private person (hence my massive distaste for the practically all-skin cutout of me) but I don't mind everyone knowing. I'm not thrilled they know we were getting dirty in the office, but them knowing in general is a moot issue now. In fact, maybe it's a positive. Maybe this will finally get Calista back into the studio.

Surprisingly, Anna doesn't call Calista out in her email. In fact, it was the exact opposite, where it appears as though she carefully crafted every sentence and paragraph to only put Calista in a positive light. Though I can't for the life of me figure out why. From where I stand, looking in on everything from my position, slightly on the outskirts of whatever went down between the two women, Calista was more in the wrong than Anna. Dangling money in front of her like that, insisting her staff was deceiving her left and right and only Anna could help her. Regardless, Anna worded her message only as a tell-all about herself with hopes of redemption. If she has any desire for eternal damnation for Calista for putting her up to it, you couldn't tell.

On my way back to the lobby, I hear the women talking around the desk. I stop where I'm at and listen in on their conversation. Maybe I'm paranoid, or maybe it's a consequence of having been lied to by Anna, but I feel the need to hear what they really think without taking my feelings into consideration. I want the truth.

"I can't believe she was able to keep up a lie like that for so long," I hear Lyric say. Her voice filled more with awe than malice.

"She did what she had to do. I did something similar last week," Nautica says. I can't see them, but I know these women well. Florence is likely on her computer still working throughout the biggest drama to ever hit the studio. Lyric is giving a skeptical but interested look. All while Mel, Grace, and Lux are not convinced and are speaking over each other to tell Nautica how she's full of shit.

"No, seriously." Nautica's voice rises and the rest fade

away. "It was during the heatwave last week; I was up at six for my morning walk while Jay has the baby. I just do a few laps around the block so I can listen to my audiobooks and not really pay attention to where I'm going. Last week while I was walking, this woman pulled up next to me, so I pulled out my earbuds and she told me she'd lost her dog and she was doing laps around the surrounding blocks to find him. The dog rarely wandered very far away. I told her I hadn't seen him. I noticed her little boy was in the back and was ready to cry, so I got her name, Amy, and her phone number and told her I'd be on the lookout for him. I'd call her if I saw him."

"Why? You don't like kids or dogs," Florence says, her fingers working that keyboard hard enough that I could hear down the hallway.

"I really don't! And it was early and too hot already; but I was listening to a really cheesy, feel-good kind of book, or maybe it was the post-baby hormones I'm still navigating. I don't know why I was so determined to help them, but I was. So, they drove off, and I put my earbuds back in and kept walking. Honestly, I slipped right back into the plot of the book and forgot. And then, I don't know how much time had passed, but enough I guess, because I saw Amy driving towards me again, but this time with the dog in the passenger seat."

No one can see me, but I'm making a what-the-fuck face trying to decipher how this relates in any way, and if I know Florence the way I think I do, she's making the same expression.

"Nautica, at what point–" Florence says before Nautica cuts her off.

"It's coming. I promise. Again, I'm listening to a Hallmark-Channel style book and I'm in a sappy happy ending mood so I yanked my earbuds out and started walking out to the car, so excited she found her pup. She stopped. Her windows were already down, so I leaned into the passenger side window and gave the pooch a quick pet and even gave it a kiss on the head. I know! I don't understand it myself. I don't like dogs, and I kissed this random one on the head before mumbling into its fur how happy I was to see him.

"Now, it's at this point I notice Amy is giving me a weird look, and is in fact not Amy. Her hair is now brunette instead of blonde, there is no kid in the backseat, and this is a blue van instead of a gray one."

The laughter that comes barreling down the hallway is infectious and I have to cover my mouth to hold in my own. Such a Nautica move. I love the woman to death, but sometimes she's almost unbelievably unaware of the world around her.

"The woman said, 'Do I know you?' and I could see the pure terror in her eyes even though she was trying to play it cool while a strange woman was practically climbing into her car to accost her dog."

"That's not–"

"Relax, Florence. The story's not over yet. Unfortunately. I panicked, and I considered telling her what had happened and we would both have had a laugh about it, but then her face was so worried that it threw me off and I just muttered out, 'I don't know.'"

Teasing groans and criticisms come from the crowd.

"And then her fear turned to concern, and she was out of her car, just randomly parked it in the middle of the road as if people in the city were going to stand for that, and she was around the hood and next to me, her eyes checking my pupils."

"Nautica, this is insane," says someone at the desk. Possibly even a client since I can't place the voice.

"It gets worse. Turns out she thought I had heatstroke, and I didn't say no. I felt like I really did have heatstroke because I got all clammy and my brain stopped working. I just stared dumbfounded as she called 911 and told them all my symptoms. Sometimes I shook my head or nodded, or did a mixture of both, which only made things worse."

Nautica detailed out how the EMT who showed up was really cute and so sweet with how he was worried about her, and so was the woman who was still there and holding the dog, who looked equally concerned. It was all just too much. She got an IV, and they put all sorts of cold packs on her to cool her down. In the end, she didn't tell anyone. They assumed she was on the brink of overheating and they caught it just in time thanks to the savvy woman–a tourist who happened to be lost, which is why she was driving so slowly down the road to begin with.

"So yeah, it's not exactly the same, but I get how things spiral out of control and then you end up just going with it and hoping for the best."

It's the reminder that I needed. These people are my work family. If I need to be around anyone right now, it's them.

"Did you catch all that, Luke?" Florence asks when I walk back into the lobby. She must have the video screens up on her computer.

Sheepishly, I nod. "I wanted to hear what you all thought about it, without me in the room."

"Oh, Luke. Anything we'd say behind your back we'd say to your face," she assures me.

"Well…" Lyric asks, not giving a damn about how I was listening in on their conversation because all they really want to know is if I read the email and what I thought of it. I should have known Anna and I weren't being nearly as discrete as we thought we were. There wasn't a monthly bet going on in the studio for July, but now I'm wondering if there actually was and it was whether Anna and I were sleeping together.

"None of you have a problem with any of this?" I ask. "She lied to all of us." I should probably be more supportive of my girlfriend (ex-girlfriend? I don't even know what we are/were). But every time I think I'm over it or can be over it, shit like this spills out of my mouth before I even realize it's happening.

There's a collective head shake and various answers of "no," "not really," and "it's complicated, but mostly no."

"But *we* weren't sleeping with her," Mel adds. "Were we? Lux?"

Lux is taken aback, but the potential additional scandal intrigues everyone else at the desk. Florence's fingers pause over the keys, her attention locked in on Lux's response.

"Me? No. Why? Did she say something?" she asks, playing with her hair and trying to hold back a smile at the prospect that she maybe had a coworker crushing on her and hadn't realized it.

Florence sighs. "It was only you, Luke. And you're welcome for that. I've basically been forcing the two of you together since the beginning." She ticks off her fingers as she relays her weeks of matchmaking: "That first class Mel was supposed to be Anna's mentor, but I made a few changes in the schedule for it to be Luke instead. I said it was per Calista, but it was just me."

"You lying bitch; I thought Calista was pissed at me," Mel says, with zero contempt in her voice.

Florence is on a roll. She ignores Mel's comment. No time for reflection on past transgressions; no time to defend herself.

"Remember, I told you I thought she was in the witness protection program so that you'd ask her a bunch of questions to get to know her better?"

"That's–" I say, not even sure how to communicate how ridiculous of a claim that is.

"Necessary," she says, completing the sentence I left hanging. "Men are terrible at getting to know women. I helped set it all in motion. Again, you're welcome, you ingrate."

My phone vibrates. It's Calista.

Where are you? Can you come to my condo?

Turns out I'm equally terrible at picking up cues from stat-uesque doormen.

On my way

CHAPTER 26
LUKE, SUNDAY, JULY 27TH

Herman lets me in, and it's as if this morning never happened. The man is a master of stoicism. I am not. I give him a thorough *what the fuck* look as I walk in while still saying thank you for him opening the door because I'm not a complete monster.

The condo door is propped open so I walk in. It's completely empty. Whatever life was here before, it's gone now. Back to the blank white slate, ready for someone to paint, decorate, and make it their own so that aside from the layout of the floors, you wouldn't even know you were in the same space. Years of living, erased.

"Out here," Calista calls from the balcony, as if I couldn't find her amongst the nothingness of the condo.

There's a built-in stone bench, and she's perched on the left side, waiting for company. I'd never noticed it before, tucked in with all the patio furniture.

My footsteps sound too loud as they echo through the nothingness. It's getting muggy out the closer it gets to noon, but I'm glad to be outside, where any and all excess noise (like my hollow-sounding steps) is swallowed up by the cacophony coming out of the city.

"Do you hate me? Does everyone hate me?" she asks in a small voice that doesn't match my big sister's usual energy. She's wearing a sun hat and oversized sunglasses as she looks out to the building across the street and the bit of water we can see over to the right.

"Hate's a strong word." I sit down next to her and look out over the balcony wall, trying to see what she's seeing, trying to understand whatever perspective she has that's instigated all this nonsense.

"I'm sorry, Luke. I've been under a lot of pressure. The alcohol–it was only supposed to take the edge off. I didn't mean to overdo it and ruin your night."

"You didn't ruin my night," I say, unsure if I believe it or not.

I turn and look back at the empty condo behind us.

"What's going on, Cally?" I ask, using the nickname she had way back when I was a kid. "Are you okay? Did you lose the condo?"

I pictured myself walking over here, giving her wholly hell while she was sprawled out on the couch, nursing her hangover. I'd tell her how she was ruining everything at the studio and she was going to lose it all if she didn't get her shit together. Now I wonder if I'm too late. Maybe it's already gone and I'm only now catching up to what I'd turned my back on for the past I don't even know how many months.

"I didn't lose the condo; I sold it."

I give a slow nod, relieved that things aren't quite as bleak as they could have been. Calista continues to stare out over the balcony, unaffected by what she's said or what's happening with the condo.

"Is that what you've been doing? When you weren't at the studio, you were selling the condo and moving everything out?"

She shrugs. "That was more recent. My neighbors bought it, all cash. It went through quickly." She readjusts her legs and her position overall, and even with the giant sunglasses and sunhat, I can see her wincing in pain.

"I also spent some of the time finding a new place to live. Somewhere down south."

"South? Like Staten Island?" She sees me now and chuckles at my expression. My blatant dislike for the location she's chosen as her future home is written all over my face.

"No, I mean south like South Carolina. Somewhere it doesn't get too cold."

I shake my head. Never in my life have I heard Calista even hint that she's unhappy living in the city. Now she's moving after what sounds like a split decision?

"I know this is going to be a lot to take in, and it's going to sound like I'm making an impulsive decision, but I need you to trust me on this."

I study her face and everything about her. She doesn't look different to me, but this conversation feels different. I nod, hoping that I'll actually trust her once she lets me in on what's happening.

"I'm not well. That sounds so generic and stupid, but I don't know how else to say it. I don't know why I'm hurting or having health issues, and I honestly can't say for how long because it's intermittent and once it lets up or goes away, I would just kind of forget I ever had any issues. I'd brush it off as some fluke, not worthy of my time worrying about it.

"When I was in college, the doctors said it was depression; sometimes the mind is so sad it physically hurts in the body, too. I got meds, I felt better, the for the most part, and I went on with my life. I still hurt in my lower stomach and down in my legs, but not enough that I couldn't keep going, keep pushing and working for everything I wanted. I even thought everyone felt like I did. That's why they say success takes hard work and it's difficult to achieve. I didn't know the average twenty or thirty-something year old didn't hurt every day."

There's a lump in my throat. Our age difference prevented us from being the type of siblings who bonded over mocking our parents' bad jokes, calling each other for help or support, or being that one person you could always count on because they were family. That closeness came later in life once I was an adult working at the studio. But even then, I had no idea. She hid it all so well.

I take her hand, sandwiching it between my own, as if I can shield her from everything that's wrong by enveloping her one hand. A tiny, pathetic gesture, but it's all I have.

"I'm not dying, if that's what you're thinking."

I love how women have some sort of psychic ability. I can't get the words out, but it's all I'm thinking, and I'm eternally grateful she could save me from my own spiraling thoughts.

"Okay. So then this is all temporary? You're going down there for a few months, see a bunch of doctors, and then you'll move back up here? Come back to work?"

She swallows and takes a deep breath, in and out through her nose. "I can't do pole anymore. And I don't want to. I mean, I do. I would do just about anything to have the life I had a few years ago. But I don't have that life or body anymore. I'm so tired. All the time. Think of the most tired you've felt, and then imagine that's your normal. Because it is for me."

It's my worst nightmare, and my sister's been living it, silently struggling, so no one was the wiser. I can't imagine not being able to let out my anger, annoyance, or even pure excess of joy by spinning and jumping around on the pole. How do every-day people survive the ups and downs of life without it? I don't envy Calista's journey in finding out.

I shake my head, still not ready to simply accept that the only viable solution for Calista is selling her condo and giving up pole dancing.

"You already said you don't know what the diagnosis is.

What happens when you move your life down there and the doctors figure it out, give you some magical pills, and then you're cured? I don't think you've thought this through, Cally. Email your neighbor. Tell her you made a mistake."

She smiles, big enough that her tears are derailed and forced to find an alternate path around her raised cheeks.

"That would be amazing, but it's not how this sort of thing works. I've already seen a bunch of doctors up here, Luke. They all say it's probably in my head or that I'm exaggerating my pain. And, even if they do figure it out, who's to say there is a cure?"

I still have her hand in mine. Her calluses are already gone. How quickly the body adapts and then re-adapts. The condo is already stripped. It's sold. Gone. She's probably already got a place down in South Carolina. It's suffocating, taking in all the changes with no chance of preventing or undoing any of it.

"I don't understand. I never… You never…"

Calista says her physical illness–her limbs and muscles that have given up on her and refuse to keep up with the physical life-style she's loved–has been an ongoing issue, but I don't have any recollection of it. It's like watching a movie with a twist at the end and you scramble to remember all the brief hints and clues that alluded to what was always there in the background, if only you'd known to watch for them.

She gives a cocky head nod. "I know. I was a master at hiding it. It doesn't help that I feel like the doctors I've seen have all gaslighted me into thinking it's all in my head. There wasn't any other choice but to push through it before. And I could, back then. But then things got worse, and it felt so good to stop pushing."

I have no words. I feel grossly inadequate as a brother right now. I know it's sexist as hell, but as the brother I'm supposed to be watching out for my sister. What the hell kind of protector was I?

"I went back and forth with good days and bad days. Most nights, I was in literal tears in bed, my lower body raging against me for pushing it so hard earlier. The worst was when I was training Anna. It sounds sick to be thankful or feel lucky right now, but I felt that way all last month. I had to teach Anna Pole 101, and mercifully my body allowed it. Mostly. I had to cut it short in the end; whatever glitch that allowed me to train, it switched up again. Like a person with dementia, each day was different, sprinkled with good times, but those became more infrequent. The bad days increased in frequency and intensity. By the end of June, I was ready to leave it all behind. And I wasn't even sad about it. The thought of not hurting so much and not being exhausted all the time was such a relief to me. I miss dancing, but I don't miss the way it started to destroy my life."

Like a mantra, my brain keeps repeating, keeps screaming about how unfair this is because Calista is too young for any disease that's akin to dementia, that's as debilitating as whatever this is. I look at her now, noting how her hands don't yet have the large veins of an older person, and her face is relatively unmarked. She always took such good care of herself.

"How can you be so calm about this?" My voice is shaking. She's imploding every aspect of her life, and here she is, sitting on her empty balcony and talking to me like this happened years before and she's merely recapping some random difficult time in her life, her indifference adding to the already muggy, suffocating air around us.

She opens her mouth to speak, then closes it. With a weak smile, she turns to me and says, "You think I'm being calm? Did you see me last night?"

"You had a few too many drinks..."

Calista leans back to give a proper guffaw at my comment and I can't help chuckle a little with her.

"I had an entire liquor cabinet. I literally looked at my still-full liquor cabinet–I was supposed to finish it off with

Paige when I said my proper goodbye to her–and I dove in. I got so blazing drunk I sat in my empty apartment in hysterics, calling Herman and telling him not to let anyone see me like that, then I continued to drink through my sobs, threw on some sunglasses to hide my red eyes, and dashed out to catch your competition."

She's still turned towards me, but all I see is my face in the reflection of her glasses. I look a hot freaking mess; I quickly adjust my expression so I don't look quite so horrified.

"I made my decision in January. First of the year. Promised myself that this would be the year I stopped hurting and stopped fighting through the exhaustion. By then I'd had my period for over a month. Heavy bleeding with crippling cramps the entire time. I was so done with it all. And then it stopped, and I felt foolish that I'd almost given up. A few weeks later it repeated. The entire process. And then again. I'm not okay, even when I feel like I kind of am. My body needs a break; I need time to see doctors. According to Reddit, I need to go through what's likely going to be months or years of testing. Figure out what's wrong, get it fixed or at the very least medicated, and then I can think about coming back. But even then, I don't think I want to."

I don't understand, but I nod.

"I might look calm now, but that's the medicinal marijuana, the hangover from last night, and shooting pain in my pelvis that are all working together to subdue me. But last night? No one would have called me calm."

More nodding without understanding. I'm not sure anyone can truly know something like this until they've lived it. I have a million questions, but it feels wrong. I hear them in my mind and they sound accusatory and petty: Has she tried better local doctors here? Has she tried getting more sleep or minimizing how much dancing she does?

No. I can't ask or say anything like that. Any hint of it

being her fault or preventable and manageable if she'd only done this and that instead? It's the last thing she needs.

We sit in silence for a while, long enough that by the time she speaks again, the shadow that previously only covered my foot is now covering half of my thigh and my hands, still holding onto hers.

"I have a favor to ask; an unfair one, unfortunately, but if there's anything I've learned from all of this, it's that I need to put myself first more often. Me, not the business."

"Anything."

"I need you to run the studio. Everything. I can't be a part of it–"

"No," I insist, shaking my head to further emphasize how I'd said anything, but had not actually meant it. I know my sister. Or at least I think I do. This is a phase; one she will immediately regret within a few weeks. While I could play along knowing she will be back, I think it's best we skip all the in-between stuff where I'm temporarily running, and possibly fucking up, the only thing in her life she's ever really cared about.

We haven't spoken to our mom's side of the family since Aunt Lonnie's illness and death all those years back. Aunt Lonnie had a series of strokes, quick in succession, that deeply impacted her quality of life. My aunt and uncles on that side of the family mourned for all of a minute before starting to fight with each other over who would be the executor for her estate. Some even insisted on putting her in hospice even though her doctors said she wasn't there yet and could still recover.

I remember Mom and Dad sitting at the kitchen table late at night. Calista had already moved out, and they must have thought I was shut away in my room or asleep because they spoke candidly. My mother was crying, gut wrenching sobs, while Dad tried to console her. "I can't believe they'd do this," she said, referring to her family's heartless actions as they all fought to get the biggest piece of her inheritance.

I texted Calista from the top of the stairs where I was hiding and listening in on my parents' discussion, and we ended our texts promising we'd never do that to each other. Those were the promises of two people who had never had money to gain or lose. We are not those same two people anymore, and I can't bear risking losing more family to fights about money or business.

Calista gives a hollow laugh.

"It's already happened, Luke. I haven't been in the studio for weeks. I've been passing more and more responsibilities to you without following up–"

"That's not the same–"

"It's been in motion since January. Maybe I should have involved you more in the transition—"

"You think?!" Her voice has remained steady while mine has escalated into panic. "I'm not some kid you need to shield from things. I'm adult enough to run the studio but not enough to be let in on it at the beginning?"

Her hangover or lack of energy keep her from arguing back. Instead, she speaks to me in the same tone she's always used for everyday conversation.

"You would have tried to talk me out of it. Just like you're doing now. I barely had the energy to keep up with my classes and train Anna. I couldn't fight against you, too."

After a stretch of silence, she says, "I had my concerns. I know in the past you've used the studio for other activities."

I feel the heat of shame rising up my neck and over my face. I'd like to argue that was a long time ago, but three years isn't very long at all.

"I know that's not who you are anymore. Not to sound too much like a parent, but it's been wild these past few years. Watching you learn it all: pole, the business, instructing, and then seeing you do it better than I ever could."

"No–"

"Yes. You can't argue with it. Like I said, it's already happened."

The shadows continue to move as we have the conversation we should have had months ago, maybe even years ago, with all the health stuff she's been hiding. I can't be too mad about it, though, because I know she's right. I would have subtly fought her the whole way. I'd have refused to accept that anything, even undiagnosed and unmedicated medical issues, could keep Calista out of the pole studio.

"Put yourself in my shoes. If your body wouldn't let you do pole anymore, would you still be at the studio every day handling all the tech aspects of the business, watching everyone else doing what they love and knowing that you can't? You'd be stuck behind the computer, on the sidelines in perpetuity."

"I can't put myself in your shoes because I'd do it anyway. I'd push myself to keep doing it because I love it."

She pulls her hand back and adjusts herself on the bench. It was a nice spot to sit for the first ten minutes, but anything longer than that gets uncomfortable with nothing but unforgiving brick pavers holding us up.

"You say that. Everyone else will say that, too. *I* said the same thing when it all started getting worse. I'll just power through. But at some point, willpower alone isn't enough. Did you hear what I said? I get my period now for months at a time? Months. Now and then I get a few days or weeks of just spotting, maybe a clear week or two in a row if I'm lucky, but right after, it rages again. To where I have to change pads and tampons in the middle of the night. Have to use an alarm to wake me up so I don't wake up in the morning looking like I'm in the middle of a crime scene."

The women at work talk freely about periods and cramps and everything that goes with it. From what they've said, I can't imagine a life where that's ongoing, the new normal. And I've never heard it being that extreme.

"And the doctors don't believe you?" There's a hint of disbelief in my voice. How is it possible that multiple doctors assume she's lying?

She shrugs. "Some think I'm exaggerating. Some said it's all part of being an older woman. One said it's probably menopause or early menopause and I'd get through it. One suggested there's a slight possibility it could be endometriosis, but the only way to diagnose is through surgery. He also said there's no cure, so there's no point in diagnosing."

Now I'm on the verge of tears.

"Don't feel bad about it. You didn't know because I didn't tell you."

Again, I nod even though it's only a formality. I don't agree with or understand any of it.

Speaking of not understanding any of it. "Why did you think people were stealing from the studio?"

"Oh, right." At this, she's smiling again, almost laughing even. "The cramps and pelvic pain get intense sometimes, so I started taking gummies to self-medicate the pain of that on top of everything else. Some time in February I was so high. So freaking high, just floating above the couch while I watched reruns of *Dirty Money* with Roderick. Which, let me tell you, being high on gummies is the only way I could sit through hours and hours of that wretched show. Roderick loved that shit. I know, I know. You never liked him anyway."

She stops talking and presses her lips together, looking off to the side and cocking her head slightly.

"Why was I talking about Roderick?"

I notice a crinkle of a gummy wrapper sticking out from the pocket of her shorts.

"I'm not sure," I say. "Something about him, pot gummies, and *Dirty Money*."

"Right. Yes, so I was watching that and thinking about

how the studio was missing some money and I got it into my mind that someone at the studio must be stealing money somehow. I couldn't get it out of my head once it was there, and it just sort of took off."

A pot gummy idea. Of fucking course that's how this all came about. They have all these programs at school about how even pot wasn't safe and had the potential to turn you crazy, jumping from the rooftops thinking you could fly. My high school friends and I had the biggest laughs making fun of those after-school specials on YouTube while we passed around a joint. But here I am dealing with the fall-out of a pot-addled poor decision.

She's laughing at herself now, so I join in. It's better than crying, which is what I'm on the verge of doing.

"I thought I was going to run some sort of spy ring."

We're both doubled over laughing at how crazy this all is.

"The next morning I promised myself I would only take half a gummy at a time going forward. But even when I was sober, the idea kept popping up. Not me being a spy or hiring one—that came months later—but finding a way to do a final once over of the business before handing it over. I thought, what if I had someone in there just checking everything out? Verifying that with my absences and my mind preoccupied with everything else going on, things hadn't gotten out of hand. And that the staff wasn't stealing from me like in *Dirty Money*."

"That's the dumbest thing I've ever heard."

"A year ago, I would have agreed with you. A few months ago, even. But my medical bills were bleeding me dry and every time I looked at our financials, they looked off to me. I was somehow convinced that solving the missing money would solve everything. Or at the very least, it was a solvable problem I could focus on, unlike all my health problems that never had solutions." She pauses, sorting through her thoughts. "The ladies at the studio can hate me if they want to, but it won't matter because you're in charge now. And I get to walk away knowing everything is as it should be. Fully staffed with the best of the best people. I'm handing you the studio on a platter. All you have to do is accept it."

"Seriously, I can't do this. It's not just the mixing-money-with-family part. I can't run a business."

Now she puts her hand on mine. "You can. I won't say I'll be there to help you along the way, because I won't. But I've already reached out to Marco, weeks ago I think, about taking you under his wing. I sent you his TikTok, didn't I? You guys didn't talk during the competition?"

So that's what her email had really been about. Not pressuring me to live up to his abilities, but a reference for how another successful studio was doing things. I consider rereading that email and trying to figure out how I'd gotten it so wrong, but it doesn't matter now. None of it does.

"No, it was a rough night."

"Hmmm," she says in response. She reaches into her pocket and pulls out her phone, her gummy wrappers falling to the floor. "Another email. From Anna."

I reach for my phone, but I don't have any notifications. I watch Calista as she reads; similar to her doorman Henry, her expression gives away nothing. The hat and sunglasses shielding a significant portion of her face makes it that much harder to read her reaction.

"What did she say?" I ask once she starts tapping on her phone again.

"I forwarded it to you. But essentially she said she's taking the next week off. Giving everyone time to figure out how they feel about what happened."

In my haste to open the email, I fumble around with my phone, ultimately sending it crashing down onto the unforgiving pavers below.

"Luke," Cally says in her most gentle voice. Her hands cover mine as I keep trying and failing to type my code in correctly. "Luke," she says again, maintaining her patience. Those gummies really do mellow her out, possibly too much.

"Let her go," she says. "It doesn't have to be forever. Just give yourselves a few weeks. Maybe a month or two."

I hold my finger up, asking for a few minutes to consider as I read the email for myself. It's nothing like the email she sent to everyone else. It's concise, formal, and there's little to nothing to be inferred from it since there's nothing of substance in between the lines. She doesn't mention me, but I know I'm the problem. Half of the staff have replied all to her email with comments about feeling slighted or mildly hurt, but mostly about how they don't care and love working with her. Whatever name she wants to go by is fine by them. Her break is from me, because I refused to hear her out and instead stormed out of her apartment like a petulant child.

When I pocket my phone and still say nothing, Calista says, "You're going to be running everything now. Can you do that and try to fix whatever is happening between you and Anna?"

CHAPTER 27
ANNA, MONDAY, JULY 28TH

"How many sessions? If you sign up for our monthly membership, we offer a 10% discount on the sessions and a 15% discount on all merch. Not the 'Just In' rack, but everything else."

The man at the desk looks back at me expectantly. I already knew about the deal. I checked their pricing extensively and compared it to the other studios around the city, only to end up with the same conclusion: I can't afford this shit.

"Just the introductory package, please." It's five classes for $100. A freaking steal, but like the streaming companies and drug dealers, it comes at a cost. They're betting your addiction, your taste and need for their product will become so deeply ingrained in your blood and DNA that you're willing to pay any price to keep it coming.

They're right. Though I personally think I'm managing my desperation pretty well, all things considered. I'm not going back to Art of Spinning. I think we could all use some time apart. Especially Luke and me. In the meantime, I'll hop around to various studios, taking advantage of their new-member packages.

"Okay." He taps away at the computer and purses his lips, disappointed in my lack of commitment. The feeling is mutual. Like five lessons will do anything to appease my newly acquired pole addiction.

The studio is similar enough with the standard color scheme of black, white, and neon pink; there are areas for clients to put their things during classes; and now this man, Elliot, is giving me the similar rundown about respect, tolerance, and the cameras in the rooms.

He looks at my cup and says, "What's your last name, Anna?"

The déjà vu vibes would blow my mind if I could get over the fact that in these studios, I won't suddenly turn around in class and find Luke, back against the wall, watching me as if I was the only person in the room, in the world even, who mattered.

It still makes my breath catch each time my memory conjures his image, eyes devoid of any love, lust, and longing. That last time I saw him, when I begged him to stay, and he didn't.

Elliot takes down my information, swipes my card, and sends me off to one of the back rooms for the Level 3 pole class that's starting in 10 minutes.

Seventeen. That's how many times I thought I saw Luke, from the time I arrived at the studio until the time that I left.

I'm sweaty and out of breath from an amazing workout, a class where I finally achieved a perfect pole cartwheel, and I feel nothing. Paige is going to say the right things and be supportive. She'll throw an arm around me and say how she always knew I could do it and how exceptional my accomplishment is. But people who aren't in pole don't fully appreciate those milestones. They can't.

I want to tell Luke and everyone else at Art of Spinning.

Like most places in the city, there's a coffee shop within a block or two of the studio. I go in and sit, remembering other days in other coffee shops. While I sip a subpar latte, I turn my phone over in my hand, debating if now is the time to open up my emails and check for responses.

It's been over 24 hours since I sent mine.

In that time, while I've spent a considerable number of hours feeling sorry for myself, I've also developed a newfound compassion for Calista. Knowing what I know now about her circumstances, and as I sit here refusing to contact the people I so desperately miss with all my being, I get why she didn't answer me back towards the end, when I was texting about having potential information. Or rather, I get why someone would avoid all conversation and interaction with everyone.

Whatever they say in return, vitriolic or unnervingly sweet–fucking Sonya who's actually grown on me enough that I miss her, too–it can't undo what's already been done. I will always be that woman who lied to everyone.

What happens if I go into work one day with a great story about how Tabby was getting robbed at the coffee shop and I did a flip over the counter to disarm the robber? No one's going to believe that. I win $500 on a scratch off but lost the ticket before I could cash it or take a picture? They'll think it's a lie. Or they'll smile to my face and give all the right responses, but secretly will wonder if any of it is true.

Worst yet. What if someone claims I'm cheating on Luke because they *thought* they saw me out with some other guy? I'd get that look from Luke. I know it. Even if it was split-second, blink or you'll miss it kind of look. Fuck, even if I don't see the look. I'll know it was there because I have a history of lying.

My phone buzzes, pulling me out of my spiraling, despairing thoughts. It's Diesel.

I need someone to cover Hellen's closing shift

Please, I'm begging you

My original plans for the day consisted of taking two more classes at the studio, thus plowing through a total of $60 worth of lessons that I used to get for free, before heading back to the apartment to see if Paige wanted to restart yet another watch-through of *Shameless*. There's something comforting about watching other poor people when you yourself are also poor.

Anything for you, Diesel

Don't fuck with me

Be here by 4

There's a wave of relief at the promise of money and being somewhere, surrounded by people, where everything is familiar and as it has been for years now.

Unfortunately, the feeling of relief is immediately swallowed by an overwhelming sense of sadness. My limbs feel heavy even though just moments ago I was eager for two more classes, back-to-back.

I don't want to put on a cheerful face all night, pretending there's nowhere I'd rather be than Papa Pizzano's Pizza Palace, serving strangers vile American-Italian food. I don't want that restaurant to be my safe haven.

I've had an actual safe haven at the studio. I've had financial security where I felt comfortable enough to be mildly shitty to supremely shitty customers, not caring if they left me a tip or not because my bank account no longer needed every dollar possible.

My heart drops when it hits me.

I'm back in the cage.

The abrupt realization is so jarring, I make a mad dash for the door so I can vomit in the gutter. Couldn't even make it to the alley.

"You look like shit," Diesel says as I walk in the front door a quarter to four.

So much for him being grateful.

"Hellen called out with the flu," he says as he follows me into the back. "Do I need to worry about you, too?"

"I'm fine, Diesel. My romantic life is in the toilet, but I'll put on my best smile and cheese it up with the customers, as always. I promise," I say, giving him my fakest smile until he relents and goes back to the front of the restaurant.

I'm about to put my phone in my locker when I feel it vibrate in my hand. Luke. It buzzes again, and again, and again. It's like that night when he fessed up to arranging a special class that consisted only of him as a student and me as the instructor. He texted over and over again, explaining it out and begging for my forgiveness.

How the tables have turned.

I would do anything to go back to that time, when the mistakes were minor and the excitement over meeting someone new was intoxicating.

Now, I feel sick; the phone is a lead bar in my hand. If Diesel could see me, he'd surely send me home, saying I was going to infect the staff and customers with whatever bug I had that was making my face pale and pasty looking.

It would be so easy to put it in the locker. Ignore the texts the same way I've been successfully ignoring all my emails.

"You've got the bar tonight," Diesel calls as he loads up a tray of plates and takes on yet another role: food runner. He spots my pathetic appearance and gives me a double-take; I smile and wave, and he rolls his eyes before lumbering back out onto the floor. Some managers try to take on an almost fatherly role with their employees. Diesel is not some managers.

Knowing I'm incapable of working while also wondering if Luke has reached out expressing his undying love to me via text, I open up my messages.

Luke: You're right. "Some distance" is probably for the best.

My stomach twists at his use of the exact same words I sent in my email to Calista. I don't regret that I sent it, and I still think it's the right thing to do, but hearing him agree hurts my heart.

Luke: Calista is moving out of the city. I'm taking over the studio.

Luke: I need to focus on that

"Trixy, or whatever the fuck you're going by today, get out there. Len's already got you on the board," Diesel says, his head poking through the kitchen swinging doors.

I put the phone in my locker, face down, as if that will somehow unsend Luke's messages. Then I grab my old familiar apron, take a deep breath, and accept that this, working full time as a server at Papa Pizzano's Pizza Palace, is my new reality. Again.

CHAPTER 28
LUKE, MONDAY, OCTOBER 7TH

"Holy shit!" I say, opening the door to the apartment. Calista already buzzed in, her voice loud and clear over the piss-poor intercom, but I'm still shocked to see her standing there.

"I know," she says, her face looking fuller than the last time I saw her, and her smile bigger than I've seen in years. "I wanted to give you more than a day's notice, but my body is still so unpredictable: some days it's intermittent unbearable pain, some days it's massive fatigue, and some days I'm relatively fine. I made plans with mom three times and had to break them. I didn't want to say I was coming until I was absolutely sure."

I press my lips together and swallow down the tears threatening to come out. If she can hold her shit together, using energy she barely has to be optimistic rather than pessimistic, I can do the same for however long she's visiting. Besides, she looks good; she feels strong in my arms when I go in for a bear hug.

"Is now not a good time?" she asks me, still in the hallway because I've forgotten to invite her in.

"Yes, yes. Come in." Calista doesn't have any luggage or bags. "Is it just you?"

She gives an all-knowing smile. "Roderick is at the hotel. He knows you hate him, by the way."

"I don't hate him." Much. Actually, my anger with him is just a gut reflex that I haven't quite squashed yet. When Calista left late in the summer, she and I talked on the phone and texted a fair amount. She told me all about their break-up, and I thought he was complete dog shit to leave her the way he did. I also blamed him for her erratic behavior before, back when I didn't know she had any medical issues. He was the ultimate scapegoat, the one I kept falling back on.

Turns out, Roderick actually left because he couldn't stand to see Cally self-medicating while simultaneously torturing herself with excessive exercise and stress that her body couldn't handle. She said they fought about doctors and what happened at her appointments, too.

Everything changed when she told him about stepping away from the studio (something he'd encouraged her to do forever ago so she could focus on her health instead) and moving down to Folly Beach, South Carolina. A few weeks later, Roderick moved down there, too. And he got a new job, one that's flexible enough for him to help with doctor appointments and hospital stays.

"Good," she says with a smile, "because he's coming to dinner with us. I already made reservations at Fushimi."

I take in her every step as she walks into the living room. She looks good. I don't see her wincing in pain, holding her lower stomach (something she used to do, though then I thought little of it), and when she sits down on the couch, she does it casually rather than carefully. She also doesn't appear to be doped up or even tipsy as she looks around my apartment.

The guys and I have been going for a minimalist look lately: DVD collection stacked on each side of the TV since we ditched all our streaming networks, a wooden coffee table complete with wooden legs versus the milk crates and sawed down door we once had, and a matching gray couch and loveseat to top it all off.

Cally's smile erupts into an outright guffaw when her gaze finally lands on my semi-nude cardboard cutout chilling between the couch and loveseat.

"You like that?" I ask, laughing along with her. "Almost had to pry it out of Lyric's cold, dead hands."

She's doubled over on the couch now, laughing so hard she's no longer making any noise at all.

I take out my phone from my back pocket and pull up Instagram. There's a hashtag for all the Channing Tatum cardboard cutout photos from Lyric's classes. It was the only way I got her to relinquish mine. Not that I was ever competing against Mr. Tatum, whose image fills my phone now, complete with random women dressed in bachelorette outfits, pole outfits, and sometimes just street clothes if they happen to walk by and hop in for a photo before slipping out the door again. All those shining, happy faces staring back at me while I scroll.

But then I think better of it and I pocket the phone again. When she calls or texts, we never discuss the studio. If she hasn't already seen Channing on our website or any of our social media, it's probably for a reason. Calista knows where to find it when she's ready.

"Why?" she manages to squeak out while I stand there speechless, taking in the return of my seemingly healthy and carefree sister. "Why?" More debilitating laughter. "Why does your crotch have a 'Hi, I'm Magnus' name tag on it?"

After dinner we go back to Cally's hotel, slowly. Roderick is the model gentleman, opening her doors and helping her in and out of the cab. If you didn't know any better, that's all it would look like. But I see it now. She needs help getting out of the cab, and she leans into him more than she normally would have. Her hand is back on her lower stomach, more so it seems as the night goes on. During dinner, she talked about how much better things are going with her doctors down in South Carolina. So far, she's been diagnosed with stage 4 endometriosis, but that only explains some of her symptoms. There are more tests to do and hopefully more treatments ahead of her so that things continue to get better. Right now, she says the fatigue is what's really bothering her more than the pain.

"Tell me about the studio," Cally says in the hotel room, not too long after she's popped a prescribed gummy. Roderick's excused himself to take a long, hot shower, so it's just the two of us again in this quaint room. There's a king-sized bed, a small sofa which I'm sitting on, and a chair that goes with a tiny desk against the wall opposite the sofa. Cally's sitting legs crossed in the chair.

"It's good," I say immediately before taking a second to assess the situation. Does she really want to get into it, or is she being polite?

We went to dinner (at a restaurant she picked out) a few blocks away from the studio and her old condo, but she didn't mention either or seem to have any interest in walking by them, so I didn't bring it up. I can't tell if she took the gummy to ease her increasing physical pain from all the activity and travel of the day, or to ease the upcoming mental pain of hearing about the past life she left behind.

When she nods with a smile, I assume it means she genuinely wants to hear the ins and outs of what's become of the business she built from scratch. Before I get into the good, I jump at the chance to say what's been weighing on my chest all summer.

"Did you know about Sonya's..." I fumble over my words. I don't want to say "secret" or "stealing" or any other of those words even though they're fitting, given the situation.

"Her off-the-books classes? Yeah, I knew."

I'd been fidgeting with my watch, but at that I freeze. I'd expected that maybe she had an inkling of *something* happening at the studio, hence her hiring Anna as some sort of mole.

She gives a soft laugh. "I'm not mad. I mean, I was. Obviously with the whole Anna thing and I had a million medical bills of my own to pay off. But now? That's all–" She waves her hand around, dismissing everything outside the hotel room. "Besides, it's not my problem anymore. It's yours."

"It's the new gummies she's on. They make her feisty," Roderick explains. He's already dressed again, his hair still slicked back and damp from his shower.

"They sure do. But you love it, don't you, Rod?"

As an answer, he crosses the short distance of the hotel room and kisses her.

"I do love it; I love you."

I check my phone while they have their moment. Rod mentions he didn't see her toiletry bag in the bathroom, and after a brief discussion they realize it's still in the car. He takes her hand in his, gives it a kiss, and then insists on going down to get it for her.

She's glowing, and I'm once against struck by how long it's been since I've seen my sister truly happy.

"He's a good guy," I say, hoping she'll believe me this time and let my past feelings about him lay to rest.

"Yeah, he really is." Then she looks down at the ground, her brow furrowed. "But we weren't talking about Rod. We were talking about the studio. And Sonya," she says, eyes wide and her smile back now that she's remembered our previous conversation. "What happened with Sonya?"

I lean back on the couch, trying to make myself comfortable for the long conversation ahead.

"I let her finish out the class she started. Then I offered to let her keep the time slot, but it has to be scheduled like the others with her hourly rate rather than a per-student, straight-into-her-pocket rate."

She exhales and shakes her head slightly. "How did that go? First official duties as the new owner and you take Lyric's cutout and Sonya's class?"

"Yeah, well, I did what you told me to do. I reached out to Marco. He helped me figure out how to word everything, and he gave me a few ideas about how to help Sonya."

She has the cockiest smile hearing that Marco, at her suggestion, helped me through it. How quickly she's forgetting that she's the one who allowed it all to happen in the first place. I won't point that part out to her, though. Like she said, it's a lifetime away now.

"So, what did Marco say?"

I tell her about the different ideas we've been throwing around. For an immediate solution with Sonya, we temporarily transformed the office into a small playroom with an Xbox in it. Sonya's kids can hang out there while she's working, and she won't have to pay for childcare anymore. Because that can't be an option for everyone at the studio, I'm working on a few other alternatives and hope to have something rolled out by the end of this year or early next. If it all works out, Art of Spinning will offer childcare services for the clients, too, and will potentially land us more clients. We'll see.

We talk about Nautica's baby, who's already all smiles and baby babbles; I tell her about my revenge pole class, which is already up to two sections a week; and I tell her about how Marco convinced me to outsource accounting and HR, and arrange for a lawyer on retainer. Since I was already making do with my current salary for the past few years, I allocated the money that used to be Cally's salary to pay for the outsourcing. Which leads us into the murky territory of having a conversation about money.

"Are you sure you don't want a percentage?" I ask for the

millionth time since that morning on her balcony when she first proposed I take over the studio. I need her to know that whatever decisions she made, they all can be undone. She can come back now, if she wants to. No hard feelings. Never any hard feelings between us.

She shakes her head emphatically. "No, no way. You've earned whatever you've made, and to be honest, it still sounds like you're still just barely getting by."

She's not wrong. I'd find a way to make it work, but I'm glad to hear she's doing okay financially and doesn't need to pull from the studio. At least not yet; the option will always stand.

"What about you? How's work going?"

Once Cally got her diagnosis and started on a treatment plan, her fatigue lightened up enough that she found her new calling working for a non-profit. The position is work-from-home 75% of the time with flexible hours. It's emotionally draining with the bulk of their clients being survivors of domestic violence, but she swears it's helped her find perspective. When she talks about her new career, she tells me about her days in limited detail, careful to keep the confidentiality of the clients she works with. I was skeptical at first when she told me she's just as happy working the phones as she was running the studio, but seeing her in person and hearing about her time there, I believe it now.

When Roderick returns, we move our conversation out to the balcony while he lounges on the bed and watches TV. Unlike at Cally's condo, our space is limited: she takes the tiny chair while I stand against the railing.

"So, what about Anna?" she asks as she dips a tortilla in salsa, courtesy of Roderick. A little something he picked up while he was getting her bag, since he knows how much she gets the munchies from her new gummies.

"There's nothing going on with Anna." I don't want to drag out the past. Cally's already apologized for bringing in

Anna as Jessi. It's done, and it can't be undone. But while I've forgiven my sister–my only family, given my parents and the rest of them have little interest in maintaining our familial bonds–I can't say the same for Anna.

"I don't understand how she's more culpable than I am," she says. Her voice is devoid of judgment; there's pure curiosity in the statement.

I list out all the ways Cally wasn't herself with the pain and self-medication on top of other factors, while Anna's only excuse was a lack of funds. There's more to it, but we don't have time to thoroughly get into it right now. I can see Calista's fighting for her life to stay awake even though it's only a little past nine. She nods as I talk, but it's more of an acknowledgement that she's hearing what I'm saying, not that she's actually agreeing with me.

"So, yeah. It didn't work out for us," I say, summing up my argument as to why there is nothing going on with Anna.

"I know, I know," she says, wincing as she rearranges her legs again and puts her hand on her stomach. "But that's all one mistake. A big one that lasted for weeks, but still only one bad decision. You really haven't spoken since the last time you and I shared a balcony?"

"It's complicated," I say, unconvinced by her little speech.

"Rod and I were complicated." She looks back into the hotel room. Roderick, sensing our eyes on him, turns to see her waving. He smiles back, blows a kiss, and mouths, *I love you.*

CHAPTER 29
ANNA, THURSDAY, OCTOBER 10TH

"It still feels like a betrayal of sorts," I say to Paige as we make our way to the subway station. She's heading into the office for her once-a-month mandatory in-person meeting at her company, while I'm heading to Pole Life, Marco's pole studio.

"No, don't do that," she says. "We've been over this a million times. You asked Calista for a week off of work. Give everyone a bit of space to adjust. Luke took over and permanently took you off the schedule. There is no sense of loyalty when someone cuts you out completely."

"I know, but–"

"No buts."

She sounds annoyed with me and with good reason. This isn't the first time we've had this conversation. I've been going out of my way finding random studios with introductory pricing, and Paige has made her criticisms well known: I should get over my pride and reach out to Luke to ask for my job back, or at the very least, not go out of my way to avoid their competition at Pole Life.

"Okay, okay. I'm doing it, aren't I? I'm going to Pole Life. I'm just telling you, as my best friend, that I'm also feeling a little shitty about it. That's all. Not saying I'm going to change my mind or anything."

"Good. I'm sorry; I didn't mean to snap at you." We walk the next block in silence, taking in the cool autumn breeze and watching the little kids in uniforms riding their scooters on their way to school.

"I just hate to see you still beating yourself up over everything. You deserve happiness, Anna. You know that, right?" She grabs my hand and gives it a squeeze.

Pole Life is as standard a pole studio as all the others: the color schemes of various pinks, dark grays, and black; the list of classes available and the order you should take them; even the layout is eerily familiar with the location of the lobby, prep areas, and instructional rooms. This one even has a box of doughnuts behind the desk.

I've come to accept that every studio is going to remind me of Luke and the rest of the crew, but mostly Luke. Months later, and I'm still looking around for him. As if there'd ever be a reason for Luke to be here, of all places. The other studios, maybe. But not here. Maybe that's really what was behind me avoiding this location. It wasn't out of a sense of loyalty, but rather that I didn't see a reason to bother with it since Luke wouldn't be caught dead here.

"Hi there!" says a chipper Sonya look-alike, her fingers poised over the keyboard and ready to go.

"Hi, I'm here for the inversion class. Anna Laurier. I signed up online last night."

I drum my fingers on the counter as she pulls up my name on the computer.

"There you are..." More typing. "Just the introductory package? Usually when people sign up for the inversions class, they're pretty serious about pole."

The conversation is typical. Some places won't even let you use the introductory pricing for anything but intro classes. Makes sense. It's obvious I'm bouncing around, taking advantage of deals.

"For now," I clarify. "I'm looking for a studio that's the right fit for me; the right feel. You know what I mean?"

She cocks her head to the right ever so slightly and smiles back at me. "I totally do, but I'm sure you'll find our studio is more than a cut above the rest." More smiling.

I return the smile. "Me, too," I say, unconvinced.

"Monny," says Marco, as he comes out of the back room and makes his way towards the front desk. He looks the same as he did that day when Luke and I had watched his TikTok on repeat.

I step off to the side and busy myself with some pamphlets at the desk while I shamelessly eavesdrop.

Marco hands the receptionist, Monny, a sheet of lined paper.

"Can you use whatever program you have on here," he says, referencing her computer, "to pretty this up? Lisa just gave me her three days' notice. I need this sign up before lunch, please."

"I'll do it!" I practically shout as I knock down the lovely display of pole pamphlets I'd been mindlessly flipping through. They both look confused and I realize they think I'm offering to create the poster.

"I mean, I'd like to put in for it. Apply for the instructor position." Oh, crap. I'm now realizing I don't even know what the hell Lisa did around here. For all I know, she was the accountant or the janitor or whatever other positions exist outside of instructing.

"Sure," Monny says to Marco, taking the paper from him and turning to her computer while still keeping an ear out for whatever it is we're about to say.

"Are you a member here?" Marco asks, looking me over.

"I am now," I say, looking to Monny for confirmation. I don't wait for her to give it, though. "I'm between studios and I just signed up for your advanced inversion class, and I've heard a lot about your studio." I bite the corner of my bottom lip, already knowing what his next question will be.

Marco's ego can't help but smile at the mention that people are talking about his studio. "Really? From anyone I know?" he asks.

I clear my throat. "Luke? From Art of Spinning?"

I expect his smile to fade at the mention of his competition. Either that or no reaction at all because I'm not altogether sure that Marco thinks of Art of Spinning as his competition. That whole competitive thing might only be one-sided.

"Luke? Are you a member at Art of Spinning?" he asks, still grinning as he leans against the front desk.

I take a deep breath, careful not to show that I'm internally panicking and trying to calm myself with extra oxygen. What did I expect? That I could one day get hired as a pole instructor without people finding out my experience came from Art of Spinning? That someone would hire me without checking my references and contacting Luke?

"I was an instructor there. For a bit." Ugh, the word "bit" lingers in the air between us, but I'm helpless to take it back. Not that any other word would be better.

Monny pauses her work, her fingers resting on the keyboard and her eyes trained on Marco, questioning if she should continue to make a help-wanted sign or if he found his new instructor already.

He gives her a subtle nod, and she keeps going.

"I'll give Luke a call. He and I have become close. In the meantime, enjoy your class. Janice is one of our finest instructors."

Right. Enjoy my class while imagining all the different ways a phone call between Luke and Marco could play out.

I'm disappointed the next day when I show up and see the lovely ad in the window, letting everyone know the studio is seeking a new instructor. If there was a phone call, it clearly didn't go well.

Monny gives me a smile in recognition and then goes right back to her work. I pause for a minute, hoping she'll recall that Marco wants to talk to me and I should stay right here, waiting for him. But no one appears and I'm in the way, so I head back into the studio to get ready for warm-up stretches.

I don't know why I thought finding another position as a pole instructor would be easy. When Calista first offered me the position, I know then it was a once-in-a-lifetime opportunity. It only makes sense that it's taking months and potentially years to get another position in the industry without relocating or settling for a job with a fitness franchise.

I hold my head up high as I enter the back studio room. If I'm going to dig myself out of this hole, I need to keep at it with the pole lessons. Who knows when I'm going to get an interview; I need to be perfect when the time finally comes.

CHAPTER 30
LUKE, SATURDAY, OCTOBER 12TH

Back in July, after I texted Anna agreeing that her leave of absence would be good for everyone, I checked my phone every few minutes looking for a response. The next day, I would check it every 15 minutes, sure that she was going to text or reach out once things settled. Soon I was checking only hourly, and then I wasn't checking for her calls or texts at all. Like Cally suggested, I reached out to Marco, and I put the studio at the forefront of my mind.

It's paid off immensely with how well the studio is doing and with the excitement around the changes we're making–outsourcing some aspects of the company and working on childcare solutions for clients and employees alike.

And then Calista stopped by with Rod. They only stayed one night in the city, but it did enough damage. It's hard enough seeing Gabe and Sasha's perfect romance around the apartment, but witnessing Calista and Rod's, too, really drove it home how much I miss texting Anna, and hugging her, kissing her, holding her hand and doing all the other things that we used to do. Out on the balcony Calista said she and Rod "were complicated." And look how that turned out.

In theory, she should be miserable with her failing health, her new career that doesn't involve pole instruction, and her new apartment that's not located in New York. But she's not. She's happier than I've ever seen her, and her relationship with Roderick has more than a little to do with it.

On the subway ride home from the hotel, I caved and pulled up Anna's old text message thread, going back to the beginning and vicariously living it all over again on the brief trip.

I might have been able to rebound from it all if Marco hadn't texted days later asking about Anna. He said she signed up for a few classes, no commitment with a membership, but did really well according to the instructor. Marco verified that she'd been at my studio and then asked why she had left.

It was too much, too sudden and unexpected. I told him something had just come up, an injury in one of my classes, and asked if I could get back to him with all the information about Anna.

I wish I could say I went up to my office then, *the* office where I have some of my fondest memories of Anna, and thought things through before calling him right back. But our childcare expansion plans are lagging and the only thing in the office now is an Xbox console, a flatscreen, and a few kids hopped up on sugary snacks and the promise of at least an hour of uninterrupted gaming.

Instead, I went and sat next to Florence, which is where I am now, once again sliding my text notification to ignore when I see Marco's name pop up. He can wait a few more hours while I contemplate my next move.

"Why aren't you answering Marco?" Florence asks, her work paused and her swivel chair turned to face me.

"Why do you ask?" During my transition to owner of Art of Spinning, I talked to Florence about the interesting files on the computer detailing a new burlesque studio with only half of the staff staying on board. Turns out, she's been trying to write a screenplay thanks to the online creative writing courses she's been taking through one of the local community colleges. "It's not going to be part of your movie, is it?"

She huffs as if it's the most ridiculous thing she's ever heard, even though she let Nautica read her first draft and it's full of events that have actually happened in the studio.

"I asked you first," the woman who's old enough to be my grandmother says. Childish, yes, but a fair point.

"He has a few questions for me that I'm not sure I know how to answer. Not yet, at least."

She nods in understanding. "He's asking about Anna?" Florence shrugs when I shoot her a look. "What? He called the front desk earlier and left a message." She slides me a Post-It with an immaculately written note asking about Anna's experience at the studio.

"Did someone say, 'Anna?'" Lux asks, appearing seemingly out of nowhere. "We went to lunch together way back when. I was hungover, and she let me borrow her sunglasses. I kept forgetting to give them back and then..." She doesn't say they went to lunch back when Anna was Jessi, or that she couldn't return them because Anna left so abruptly, but she doesn't have to. We fill in the blanks for her; or at least I do.

"Luke was just about to go see her," Florence says, lying as easily as Anna used to. "Go grab them. He'll be happy to pass them off."

Lux scurries off and I bore holes into Florence's face with as stern a look as I can muster. In truth, Florence gives off too much of a mother vibe for me to effectively stare her down.

"No, no, no, Luke," she says, complete with a finger wag. "We've all allowed this Anna thing to drag out long enough. You're too chickenshit to call Marco back? That's because you don't want to. You're not ready to let her go."

Lux hands me a pair of sunglasses. I remember Anna wearing them the first time we met. She had them on the top of her head at the coffee shop and nervously adjusted them after the whole party below my belt comment.

"Go, Luke," Florence says, turning back to her computer as if the conversation is officially over.

"Go where? To her apartment? Just show up?"

Florence sighs and makes a big to-do of swiveling her chair again. "Go to Pole Life. Anna's there. Marco said he'd love an answer by four since she was going to be in the studio for a class then."

I double-check the very concise Post-It she gave me earlier and confirm none of that information is on it.

"It's all up here; I'm a steel trap. I was going to hound you about after lunch. You think better on a full stomach. Not so grouchy."

I turn the sunglasses over in my hands. I don't know what I'm going to say or how I'm going to feel seeing her in person, but it looks like I'm about to find out.

CHAPTER 31

ANNA, SATURDAY, OCTOBER 12TH

I push myself harder than necessary during our cool down stretches. Even though all I've heard from Marco is radio silence since that first day, I'm maintaining my positive outlook: as long as the sign is hanging on the front window, I have a shot at a position here.

Throughout class, I gave it everything I had. I worked closely with the other clients, trying to help them out with their moves, while also showing off my instructional skills. Does Janice have any actual pull in this studio? Who the hell knows. But at this point I'll try anything. Even tearing my muscles from their bones as I try to reach beyond my normal limits.

"Anna."

I disengage from my current stretch and look up to find Janice standing in front of me.

"Are you okay? You've been holding that pose for over five minutes," she says, watching me carefully as I sit fully upright again.

"Oh, yeah. I'm good. Just zoned out, I guess."

"Okay. I have to get going, but the room is empty for a

while if you want to keep stretching it out. Just don't get on the poles without an instructor around."

"Great. Thank you. I won't."

I go down for another deep, muscle-ripping stretch. No one will be here to see it; this one's for me.

"Hi, Janice." I hear someone say behind me.

"Hey, Luke. Are you here to see Marco?"

I freeze. It's Luke's voice. My Luke's voice. I'd know it anywhere. But me? I'm folded in half on the floor. I stay that way, hoping he doesn't realize who I am. I've been dreaming of running into him at a studio somewhere, in the park, on the streets. The possibilities are endless in this city. But those fantasies always involved me with perfect hair and makeup and an expectation of seeing him. While I currently look stunning as a lame way of trying to increase my chances of getting hired, I'm not mentally prepared. Luke was supposed to be anywhere in the city but at his competition's studio.

"No, actually. I'm here to see Anna."

I'd been staring at my shoes and ankles during my stretch, but now I focus beyond them and remember there's a wall of mirrors. I see I'm not nearly as hidden as I'd thought I was. Okay, then. This is happening.

I stand and gather my things while Janice and Luke exchange formalities. Then it's just the two of us in the studio.

"I brought your sunglasses," he says, handing me the pair I lent to Lux over the summer. "I heard you used me as a reference here, and when Lux heard… You know, it doesn't matter. You were here. I had your sunglasses. Now you have them."

He shoves his hands into the pockets of his jeans. I immediately notice the jacket and glasses and wonder if that's intentional. He knows I have a kinky soft spot for his nerdy professor cosplaying.

"Thanks," I say, feeling better already now that I have

something to fiddle with while we talk. "So, you're friends with Marco now? I did not see that one coming."

He lets out a soft chuckle. "Me either, but he's been a lot of help with running the studio and everything. He's a good guy."

I nod, unsure of where this conversation is going. His hair is shorter than I remember, or he just got it cut and it hasn't grown back yet. And it sounds like he's permanently running the studio with Marco as his mentor. So much change in so little time. Luke's growing leaps and bounds, while I feel like I'm going backwards.

"So, yeah," he says, dragging his fingers through his hair. "Marco said you're looking to fill the instructor position here."

I nod again. "It seems like a nice place. And like you said, he's a good guy. Right?" I'm not asking if Marco is a good boss; I'm asking if there's some reason, any reason at all, that I shouldn't get a job here as an instructor.

"Yeah, he's a good guy." Luke pulls at his collar and looks towards the door. "It's a little warm in here. Can we talk? Outside?"

In the short distance from the back studio room to the front door, I've figured out what I'm going to say to Luke. First, I need to tell him how much it hurt when he walked out that night. When he heard me beg him to stay, and then turned his back and left. Then I'm going to tell him how even though I'm still feeling hurt, I miss him and everyone else. Finally, I'm going to beg for my job back at Art of Spinning. Maybe if I apologize again for all the lies and sneaky behavior with Calista, he'll find a way to forgive me. If he and Marco can be besties, surely anything is possible.

Luke does his typical ladies first move at the front door and I step out onto the sidewalk. It's a gorgeous day. The sun is out and streaming through the autumnal leaves on the trees lining the city street. A good omen if I've ever seen one. I'm about to turn away from the blazing colors and tell him exactly how I feel when his hands clamp down on my shoulders and I hear him grumble a few expletives behind me.

He lets go of me and leans on the tree trunk for support, his one leg bent and hovering over the sidewalk so all his weight is on the other.

"Fuck, I rolled my ankle. So stupid," he says more to himself than to me.

I wince empathetically. I know that sharp pain, and I know that annoying realization that you won't be able to walk on your own for at least a few hours.

"Here, let me help you." I drape his arm around my shoulders and I'm hit with the realization that I haven't actually thought this through. What am I going to do? Help him hobble back to the subway? I don't even know if there's a direct line nearby to get him back to his apartment.

"Are you?" I ask. "Did you just sniff my hair?" A bit too accusatory in tone, considering I'm memorizing every inch of the feel of his body against mine, and considering that I took a large whiff myself when he first threw his arm around me.

"Yes?" he answers sheepishly.

"Come on," I say through a smile I can't squelch. "Let me get you a cab and help you back to your apartment."

We maneuver to the curb and are lucky to hail a cab almost immediately.

"It's you! And you're still together!" Our cab driver, the same one we had all those months ago, is out of the cab and helping us into the back seat as he grins ear to ear. While he's assisting Luke, he asks him about his sister, and Luke gives him the abridged version of how Calista has some health stuff going on, but their relationship is better than ever and she's feeling better as well.

Once we're settled in the back seat and the driver has the address, Luke and I pick up where we left off.

"Come back," Luke says. Just two words. He doesn't

clarify if he wants me to come back to him, or to the studio. It sounds like both. I want it to be both, but it's not that simple.

I shake my head. "I can't. We can't." It would be so simple to jump at his request, but that wasn't the plan. I swore to myself in all my imagined scenarios where I encounter Luke somewhere out in the wild, that we'd hash out what went wrong in the first place. There are reasons we haven't talked or even texted in over a month. Resuming business as usual would be nice, but ignoring our past transgressions would lead us right back to where we've been.

"I can take an alternate–"

"Yes, we know," Luke and I say at the same time. The driver rolls his eyes and carries on with the direct route.

"I forgive you," Luke says. "Everyone forgives you. We all want you to come back to the studio."

"I don't forgive you," I blurt out. It's cathartic. I didn't even realize until I've said it out loud that that's at the root of how I feel. I haven't called or contacted him, not because things would be messy or awkward, but because I haven't forgiven him. "I tried to apologize and make things right, and you walked out on me. And your face and expression and words were so hateful. Do you even realize that's my last memory of you? Walking out on me when I pleaded for you to stay?"

He's speechless. So is the driver, though I know he's listening. His eyes keep going back and forth between the road and the rearview mirror.

Luke's expression is that of an animal who's frozen in terror and awaiting the predator's next move. Clearly, I've caught him off guard.

"Every time I think about reaching out to you or someone at the studio, your angry face flashes through my mind and I can't. I saw it in my mind when I read your last text messages."

"Anna," he says softly and sweetly. I've been waiting so long to hear him say my name like that.

"I don't get attached, and this is why." I press my lips together to fight back the incoming tears. "I asked for a little time off, for some space, and you cut me out completely. And yes, maybe I should have called once things settled, but you should have, too."

He nods, but says nothing, and it's a dagger to my heart that I word-vomited every emotion I've felt since then, and all he's giving me back is a gentle nod of the head.

His hand is on the seat a mere inch or two from mine; I move my hand and put in my lap. It's his turn to put in the work to help bridge the gapping hole in our relationship.

"You're mad at me?" He asks, somewhat in disbelief. "You're mad because you think I overreacted when you told me our entire relationship was built on a lie?"

I throw my hands up in the air and the three of us, cab driver included, are all talking over each other, trying to figure out who's the most culpable for our abrupt break-up.

I keep repeating my main points from earlier while offering rebuttals to Luke's arguments. Luke is claiming he deserved more time to process the extensive lying, and how it's not fair for me to be mad at him for walking out. The driver has no clue what went down between us, but he joins in anyway, insisting we're probably in need of some couples counseling and oh, by the way, he happens to have a business card since he does that on the side.

We ignore the card he offered and continue to argue until we pull up to Luke's apartment building. Luke insists on paying the fare and I don't even pretend to insist we split it or that I pay instead. But I do get out and help him out of the cab, too. The driver was more than happy to help us in, but I think we've thoroughly annoyed him since and he's ready to move on to his next fare.

He mutters a few words to us about how it'll never work,

but he wishes us the best of luck anyways. Then he's out of our lives once more and we're hobbling into the building and up to the eighth floor.

The fight is out of us once we're in the elevator. He's leaning against the wall, and I'm standing in front of the doors, watching the lights go up one floor after the other. It's like a reverse countdown to when we'll walk out of each other's lives, this time probably for good.

"How's Sonya?" I ask. Ever since that night at the competition, when I glimpsed what can only be described as Calista's evil alter ego, I've been worried about what would happen when it inevitably came out that Sonya was running secret night classes.

I don't look at him, but I can hear the hint of amusement in his voice. "She's good. We set up temporary child care in the studio for her and put all her classes in the official schedule."

I try to see him in the reflection of the doors. They're no mirror, but the metal offers a smeared, fuzzy outline and I see he's facing me. I should turn and meet him head on, but I can't bring myself to do it. Instead, the doors open and I brace myself for one last embrace as I help him into his apartment.

It's cleaner than I expected. I was joking with him before when I made the literary frat house comment, but I guess a part of me really expected frat-style living conditions with three guys living together. Like a milk carton or cinder block coffee table or something like that.

"Ahhhh!" I scream, clutching my chest in pure horror when I see the half-naked man in the corner.

Luke screams too, but it's because I jerked in response, and in an effort to catch me, he put all his weight on his bad ankle.

I quickly recover when I realize it's just a cutout of Luke and not an actual naked intruder. "Shit. I'm sorry. Why would you have something like that in your apartment? Or at all?" I don't mean to, but I'm outright laughing now, even though he's still wincing in pain and leaning on the couch instead of me. I clamp my hands over my mouth to hide my laughter, but there's more and I have to comment on it. "And you've named your own cock Magnus?" I ask through my fingers.

He's smiling now, though it's still more of a grimace. "It's a long story. Just know that Calista and Lyric were involved."

I nod. That sounds about right. I'm relieved to hear it wasn't the result of a girlfriend, and I don't see any hints of a woman living here, but there's an empty feeling in my gut from seeing the cutout and not knowing the backstory. I'm not a part of that life anymore.

"Luke," I say, my voice cracking. "I'm sorry I never called." He was right, what he said in the cab. I was arguing back, but I heard what he said, too. Heard his side of things with how I took so many steps back from him and the studio, and then I never reached out again.

"I'm sorry, too." He takes off his glasses and pinches the bridge of his nose. He's sitting on the arm of the couch while I'm leaning against the wall across from him. "I should never have left that night, and I shouldn't have let work take over my life."

Luke holds out his hand, and just like that first night after class when he helped me off the couch, I instinctively take it. Except this time, after a gentle pull, I'm in his arms in as proper an embrace as you can have when the other person has a newly injured ankle and is favoring it. A few minutes ago, I was convinced a lifetime of memories and changes had happened since I last saw him, but this feels like home again. This feels like nothing's changed.

My fingers rake through his hair. It's shorter, but the sensation is the same, the feel is just as I remember it, and the sigh he lets out as his head tilts back tells me we're picking up right where we left off.

"Anna," he says as his hands slip under my shirt so his

firm, calloused hands are gripping my sides, his fingers gently massaging my back muscles. "I should really ice my ankle."

"Oh, crap. Yes. Yes, we need to do that right away." When I pull away, we do that adorable thing where we hold hands as long as we can until only our fingertips are touching while our arms are outstretched. Then we're separated and I'm rummaging through the kitchen for a towel and ice pack, while Luke is using the couch as a crutch as he makes his way to what I'm assuming is his bedroom.

"Hold on; I'm coming," I say, reaching once again to drape his arm over my shoulder.

We take care of business first. I set up a pillow at the headboard for him to lean against, and I place the other pillow at the end of his bed for his foot to rest on while he's icing it. Then I nestle in next to him with my head on his chest while he uses his phone to look over his scheduled classes for the next few days to see which ones he'll need to find coverage for. In the process, I get added to the schedule as well, and Luke sends a sorry-not-sorry email to Marco informing him I'm now unavailable to take on that instructional position at Pole Life. I send a similar text to Diesel about how I'm cutting my hours back again.

With all our responsibilities out of the way, we lay in Luke's bed, which smells deliciously like him, and talk for hours before finding ourselves getting tangled up in his fragrant sheets. Well, as tangled as one can get with a newly sprained ankle. But we make it work and it's refreshing to be in bed for once.

ALSO BY LEIGH DONNELLY

Spicy Rom-Coms

Once You Cross That Line

Ignore Scott

Loathe Gray

Fake It Till You Make It

Women's Fiction

It Was Always This Way